Early Praise for *Choose Love, Not Fear*

"Every leader should read this book! Gary and Ryan Heil have distilled the essence of great teams and great leaders into a few short, but profound principles. Choose Love, Not Fear *shows a unique and compelling way to build exceptional organizations. Wisdom on every page."*

Admiral William H. McRaven, U.S. Navy (Retired); Former Commander of the US Special Operations Command and former Chancellor of the University of Texas System

"Great leaders create great teams, and with Choose Love, Not Fear, *Gary and Ryan show how creating a human-focused culture is the only way to win the future. Deeply researched and filled with inspiring examples, this book is an essential handbook for today's leaders."*

Arianna Huffington, Founder and CEO of Thrive Global

"Every few years, we need to be reminded of the truth that when leadership conflicts with human virtue, something is wrong with leadership. Choose Love, Not Fear *is such a reminder, and it couldn't come at a better time. Read this book and apply it—you will be happier and more successful for all the right reasons."*

Arthur Brooks, PhD, Professor of the Practice of Public Leadership, Harvard Kennedy School; Arthur C. Patterson Faculty Fellow, Harvard Business School

"In compelling and inspiring fashion the Heils describe the importance of building a culture of respect and trust in which people are fully engaged and share in a common vision; the importance of believing in yourself and believing in your team. Leadership is clearly a choice. Choose to lead from love, not fear."

Pamela Landwirth, CEO, Give Kids the World Village

"Gary and Ryan Heil have issued a clarion call for a new approach to leadership in our offices, classrooms, and playing fields. They show that relying on intimidation and control is not only inhumane—it's also ineffective. The very best leaders today must embrace intrinsic motivation, vulnerability, and, yes, love. Fear, we now know, makes us dumber. This remarkable book will make you smarter."

Daniel H. Pink, #1 New York Times bestselling author of *DRIVE*, *WHEN*, and *TO SELL IS HUMAN*

"Love. Humility. Service. These are the fundamental attributes of great leaders. In Choose Love, Not Fear, *the authors challenge us to turn the rhetoric of good leadership into action—to find the courage to make the choices necessary to build cultures founded on positive emotion that make high levels of engagement possible. A must-read for leaders at all levels."*

Alan Mulally, Former President & CEO, the Ford Motor Company and Boeing Commercial Airplanes

"I've worked with the Heils for more than a decade. Their passion for understanding what makes a great leader has inspired me. This book uncovers what today's leaders must focus on!!! Fascinating read."

Mark King, CEO, Taco Bell, former President of Adidas North America

"Sparked by wisdom, intelligence and deep insight into human nature, this book provides a masterful framework for building great teams. It should reach the widest possible audience."

Doris Kearns Goodwin, Pulitzer Prize winning historian

Choose Love, Not Fear

CHOOSE LOVE NOT FEAR

HOW THE BEST LEADERS BUILD CULTURES OF **ENGAGEMENT** AND **INNOVATION** THAT UNLEASH HUMAN POTENTIAL

GARY HEIL | RYAN HEIL PhD

Choose Love, Not Fear:
How the Best Leaders Build Cultures of
Engagement and Innovation
That Unleash Human Potential

By Gary Heil and Ryan Heil

Published by CFIL Publishing, Hershey, PA (www.CFILpublishing.com)

First printing, October 2019

Project editor & advisor: Laura Pyne
Cover design: Klassic Designs
Interior design: Benjamin Vrbicek

Hardback ISBN: 978-1734105100

Printed in the USA
Signature Book Printing, www.sbpbooks.com

Contents

Foreword

Dabo Swinney | Head Football Coach, Clemson University

"What does love have to do with building great teams?"

For me, the answer is simple. Love is the foundation of every great culture. I can't imagine building a program that sustains success through generations of players, without the people on the team loving each other. I believe that a culture built on love and not fear is necessary for a team to turn temporary successes into sustained performance in highly competitive situations.

When Ryan and Gary asked me to write the forward to their book about creating a culture that supports unleashing human potential, I was immediately ALL IN. The three of us share a belief that culture is what distinguishes great teams from merely good ones. We believe that building a culture founded on positive emotion gives every person the best chance to perform at an inspired level no matter the field of play.

At Clemson, developing a more positive culture is always on our minds. As coaches, we are constantly trying to make the environment better this year than it was last year. We are committed to making our program one that attracts great players and provides an environment in which they can get a great education, maximize their athletic potential, and learn life lessons that will make them more productive members of our communities. We believe that building environments that support our players reaching their potential is more than a job. It is our calling. It is our responsibility.

The authors have provided an excellent framework that can assist leaders and their teams in their quest to build more effective cultures. Their framework is simple and compelling. It can serve as a reminder of the fundamental human issues that must be addressed before a team can consistently play at a high level.

Gary and Ryan do not suggest that they have found a new secret leadership sauce. Instead, they demonstrate through examples and research, that much of what it takes to build more effective cultures has been known for decades. They suggest that building great teams requires that we summon the courage to build processes whose basic assumption is that ordinary people are capable of achieving greatness. I agree.

I also agree with the authors when they suggest that building great teams is a life-long, not-to-be-underestimated challenge that begins with a passionate commitment to a shared sense of purpose, one worthy of individual sacrifice. For when one person goes 'ALL IN' and chooses to sacrifice for the team, it is more likely that the next person will make a similar commitment. And, as the author's note, with each person's commitment, it becomes easier to recruit the right players and create an environment where winning is significantly more likely.

I'm not saying that creating a winning team is easy or that loving each other guarantees greatness. It's not that easy. I am saying that without players who love each other and feel connected to the team, sustained winning is unlikely. I believe that when we care deeply for each other, it is far more likely that people will feel safe enough to take the risks necessary to learn, to grow and to perform.

And we must perform. Today, most of us play in performance-driven environments. We will be judged by how well we play, by how many games we win and by how much profit we create. We should expect our performance to be evaluated. This book does not argue that caring is a substitute for winning or performance. It simply argues that caring deeply makes winning more likely and that great teams should be judged not only by the number of wins they accumulate but also by their humanity—the extent to which people on the team are willing to fully engage.

I suggest as you read this book that you keep the title in mind. Choose Love. Not Fear. Most people realize that a football player who enters the game with confidence is likely to play better. They would also say that playing in fear is a recipe for underperformance. Love over fear seems simple enough.

But in my experience, choosing love is not a common practice. Too many still seem *un*willing to recognize the power of love and connection in every endeavor from coaching college football to teaching fourth grade. We can do better.

If you believe as I do, that there is untapped greatness in each of us, I hope that you will allow these ideas to challenge you and your team to find new and innovative ways to help people perform closer to their potential. As leaders, we have the opportunity to make a significant difference in the lives of others and change the world a little in the process. To begin the process, we need only BYOG.

Best of luck,
Dabo Swinney

Clemson SC
August 1, 2019

Introduction

What Does Love Have to Do with It?

Using love in the title of a book is risky. At least that was the advice that we received from some of the most experienced editors and communications professionals in North America. They were convinced that using love in a leadership book made it more likely that we might be dismissed as providing a point of view that is too touchy-feely, or straight out of Never-Never Land. Most tried to be gentle as they cautioned us, but their message was clear: "Don't do it." For them, talking about teams of people who love each other would not strike the right note in a world that is growing more competitive and more performance-oriented.

But we had no choice. After spending the last decade immersed in a study in which we interviewed coaches, teachers, and leaders, love best describes the feeling we had when we were in the presence of exemplary teams. The relationships on these teams went far beyond the "We care about people," or

"People are our most important asset," rhetoric that has become so common.

On exemplary teams, we found that the way people related to one another made them more willing to sacrifice for the common good. They seemed to listen more, learn more, take more risks, and treat each other with more respect. They had more empathy for each other. They smiled more and seemed to be having fun even as they remained incredibly focused. When we met these teams, people had a spring to their step, an energy that engaged us viscerally. We could feel the difference immediately. Their energy drew us closer. Their example demonstrated how love in an organization can drive out fear, broaden perspectives, and make it safe to challenge yesterday in the hope of a better tomorrow.

What does love have to do with building great teams? In the words of one exemplary leader, "Just about everything."

Why this Book? Why Now?

Today, it's not hyperbolic to say that we are in a fight for our leadership souls. At every turn, we are being challenged to choose between the comfort of yesterday's familiar practices and a more people-centric road far less traveled.

Will we choose to continue to perpetuate practices whose inevitable effect, even if unintentional, is to use fear to try to control outcomes and improve performance even though we know that the resulting fear makes us dumber, restricts what we see, and narrows what we think is possible?

Or, will we choose to embrace the notion that we can build organizations based in positive emotions that make it far more likely that we will more fully engage the human spirit on our teams?

We wrote this book because we believe that there is a better way to engage people and facilitate creative contributions. It begins with the belief that we must choose to lead from love and to reduce the unnecessary, counterproductive fear inherent in much of what was considered acceptable leadership in the past. We can no longer afford to give only lip service to building innovative, inclusive practices that are more consistent with what we know about why people make commitments on some teams and not others. Our experiences have made us true believers, unabashed advocates, of cultures that unleash the potential of people. We believe that leaders have the responsibility to create environments where helping people reach their potential is not a slogan but a commitment.

We come to this challenge with our eyes wide open. We have spent decades working with extraordinary leaders, bad managers, legendary coaches, entrepreneurs who led teams that invented new markets, and ego-driven authoritarians whose choices destroyed organizations. We have worked with former Presidents of the United States, chief executive officers, coaches in professional and college sports, high school principals, MBA students, the United States Congress, and nonprofits. These opportunities gave us a ringside seat to observe the good and the bad outcomes of many efforts to improve leadership and culture.

To be blunt, the outcomes of most efforts to help leaders build more effective cultures have been disappointing. Despite the best efforts of an army of smart people, a library of advice, and $50 billion a year in investments, most organizations seem designed to make effective leadership difficult. The unfortunate reality is that most organizations still celebrate average leadership and tolerate poor leadership.

A 2016 Gallup study found that 82 percent of leaders stink—at leading. Only 18 percent demonstrate a high level of leadership competency.[1] Yet, in a McKinsey and Company study of more than 52,000 managers and employees, 77 percent of managers responded that they believe they inspire action.[2] It appears that far too many leaders have not received the memo that describes their ineffectiveness. If these studies are accurate, leaders seem to be suffering from a kind of "motivated blindness" that leaves them unable or unwilling to alter their leadership practices.

It need not be this way. When we look closely, examples of great teams and exemplary leaders surround us. There are teams in every community that simply refuse to accept the limitations that undercut other efforts. Through example, these teams teach us that more is possible and that, in the right environment, it's natural for ordinary people to choose to be extraordinary.

Visit the best school in a community, and you will inevitably find an innovative principal and an inspired staff who play by a different set of rules. And yes, there is always that demanding teacher who consistently refuses to accept less than our best and who routinely turns a class of normal students into a team of inspired learners. When you find a great restaurant, you find a team that believes that serving others is more of a calling than a job. All branches in a bank are not the same. Even in banks that are considered average, there are branches that will blow your mind with their responsiveness and professionalism. They simply refuse to succumb to the mediocrity that characterizes the rest of the organization.

When you get to know the people on these exemplary teams, you can't help but notice their normality. They are much like us. Some are tall; others are short. Some have big personalities while others are shy. A few are charismatic. A number are good public speakers, but most of them are not. The leaders of these teams were not born with a special leadership gene, nor have they uncovered a few secrets that render them more successful. In actuality, most do hundreds of little things differently than their less successful peers, guided by a love for people, a passion for what they are trying to accomplish and a curiosity that makes them avid learners.

This book describes some of the ways that exemplary teams are different. But it is more than a list of cultural traits that distinguish great teams and great leaders from the merely good ones. It is a call to action. It is a call to choose remarkable over ordinary. It is a call to choose positive emotion over fearful control. It is a call to begin a conversation that can accelerate learning and help us transform relationships in ways that can reduce our natural inclination to resist change and stifle innovation. It is a call to broaden our leadership conversations, to challenge more people to lead regardless of position.

Perhaps, more importantly, it is a call for us to acknowledge the breadth of our responsibility as leaders. When we are successful in creating cultures that support engagement and creative contributions, we not only win more games, increase profitability, and enhance education, but we also change lives in the process. When we choose to be exemplars, when we choose to do the right thing even when the expedient thing is easier, our lives are enhanced as we fill our days with more positive emotion. When our teammates feel that they have made a positive difference, they go home and are better fathers and mothers, sisters and brothers, parishioners and citizens. As leaders, we have the opportunity and responsibility to enrich the world in immensely powerful ways.

If you believe that there isn't one right way to lead but that there must be a better way, we invite you to join the conversation.

Democratization is Narrowing Our Leadership Choices

The all-powerful leader may have been successful enough in the past. However, in today's world, that type of leader is quickly becoming a liability. The one trend in the practice of leadership that has been consistent over time is the transfer of power from those who used to hold all the power to those who, historically, have had little. Today, we stand at the brink of a digital revolution that is accelerating democratization at a pace that will render leaders less powerful.[3] That is a good thing. Leaders with an overabundance of power inhibit engagement and the expression of creativity. When leaders hold more power, people have less freedom. They have less need to be fully engaged when one person has the answer and makes the rules.

To be successful in the future, we will need less powerful leaders. The changes that we will experience in the next couple of years will be far greater than what we have experienced in the last couple of decades. We will be challenged to move faster, innovate quicker, and lead teams of people who are far less willing to follow absent a worthy cause. The changes at our doorstep will rock our world and force us to find a way to influence people more through the power of our beliefs than through our positions.

Just as Martin Luther used the printing press to gather support in his revolt against Rome and radio and television were instrumental in bringing down the Iron Curtain, recent developments in technology have accelerated the pace of change and shuffled the rules governing how people will interact. As people find new ways to share information and connect with like-minded souls, they invariably become more courageous when they realize they are not alone. Just as there is power in information, there is even more power in groups of people connected in a ubiquitously informed community. The lone voice today can find kindred spirits around the world without leaving the couch. A frustrated team member can alert a significant number of teammates, customers, and regulators in short order regardless of the accuracy of the information.

We are not saying that today's leaders are not powerful or that they are less important. We are saying that we will be required in the future to find a more inclusive way forward. We are saying that the last chapter of fear-induced, command and control leadership is being written. We are warning that, although leaders can still command compliance in many cultures, future efforts to achieve such compliance will require more power and will come at a much higher price. The methods that formed the foundation of yesterday's successes are likely to be less effective, and shifts in our leadership thinking and actions that might have been perceived as optional yesterday will quickly become more necessary as innovation becomes the most valuable currency in every endeavor from reinventing the spread offense in college football to changing the way customers connect and purchase products.

Today, many teams are still led by baby boomers (one of us), most of whom learned to challenge traditional authority much more than their parents did. But a willingness to challenge orthodoxies pales in comparison with what is coming. Millennials (one of us), those born between 1980 and the turn of the century, are here and they are different. They grew up in the middle of a communication revolution—the effects of which baby boomers often underestimate. They are capable of great commitment but won't give that commitment easily. They are likely to be less trustful and more self-confident. They are less willing to follow authority blindly and have been conditioned to connect with others while challenging the existing order. They are accustomed to being informed because, for their entire lives, every answer has been only a click away. "Informed and connected" is what they know and, therefore, what they expect.

This is all good news because if we are mindful, we will understand that there will be no effective retreat to yesterday's methods of using fear to control. We will no longer be able to pretend that when 30 percent of our team members are highly engaged, we are leading effectively. Bad leaders will finally be too expensive to support. And we will no longer be able to ignore people's need to belong to a group that is connected through a gratifying level of positive emotion.

Instead, we will need to acknowledge that times are changing and that shifts in our leadership choices that might have been perceived as optional yesterday are quickly becoming more necessary as tomorrow's most coveted recruits are demanding a different kind of culture and a different kind of leader. This book is dedicated to the development of both.

Building a More Effective Culture is Everyone's Responsibility

- Why do so many leaders talk passionately about the need to engage people and then perpetuate practices that inhibit engagement?
- Why do so many talk of the need for more inclusive people practices but choose to treat these practices as optional?
- Why do so many well-intentioned leaders fail to change even when they are convinced that change is in their best interest?
- Why do some leaders succeed at creating great teams while others struggle?

These were a few of the questions that we attempted to answer by interviewing more than 700 leaders responsible for managing transitions in a wide range of organizations. We spent the last decade trying to assess why so many leaders had trouble making the changes that they knew would enhance their abilities to more fully engage people.

Unsurprisingly, we found that most leaders had similar beliefs about the characteristics of a great leader. Most listed a set of traits that were similar to the list of leadership traits that have been admired in every civilization for thousands of years. Persistence. Empathy. Gratitude. Passion. You can finish the list. These traits are well-known, well-studied and universally appreciated.

However, when we asked these leaders how often they lived the values that they admired in others, the conversation became less comfortable. People seemed to know that, in most cases, they talked a better leadership game than they were willing to play. Most readily admitted that they frequently did not act as they believed a great leader would act. Most had excuses for their inaction at the ready.

"Have you met my boss?"

"You can't lead that way with the people on our team."

"I know that there is a better way to lead. But it is just not me."

Or our personal favorite, "Can you really make money doing that crap?"

These leaders seemed to know that there was a more effective way to engage with people even if they were unconvinced that it was a practical solution to their leadership challenges.

Most were unwilling, absent a crisis, to trust their inner voices. The unmistakable story that emerged from our interviews was that most leaders talked of the need to change but felt constrained by the pressures in their present cultures.

In retrospect, our findings that cultural pressures significantly inhibit leadership innovation should have been predictable. Nearly every cultural study in the last century has come to the same conclusion. Culture creates resistance to movement contrary to the culture. Culture, the shared values and beliefs of the group is a stabilizing force that protects us from ideas incompatible with present values and mores. The culture of a group binds it together for better or worse. It provides stability and predictability at a cost. In most cases, it protects past practices at the cost of future innovation.

If we are to succeed in our efforts to find ways to innovate faster and build more creative, inclusive cultures, we will have to become more mindful of how we have allowed our past experiences to over-influence our future choices. We can no longer afford to underestimate the challenges inherent in leading cultural change. We can no longer afford to overestimate the influence of individuals and underestimate the influence of team culture.

In the following chapters, we advocate a number of leadership choices that we believe are critical for creating cultures that better support the unleashing of human potential. We don't offer these as a list of the attributes of leaders who create effective cultures. We are convinced that a complete list of the behaviors of successful leaders *does not exist*. We understand that many of these choices have been discussed for generations. However, over the last decade, in interview after interview, we were struck by how the most effective leaders do these eight things differently than their less successful peers.

Choose Love, Not Fear

This choice is foundational; it affects all other choices. No great leader or athlete or artist or student plays well in a culture dominated by unnecessary fear.

Create a Compelling Cause Worthy of Commitment

An emotionally engaging sense of purpose can become a unifying force for a team and provide the opportunity for people to find meaning in their actions.

Get the Right People on the Team and the Wrong People off the Team

Getting the right people in the right positions and getting the wrong people off the team makes effective leadership far more likely.

Expect Remarkable

There is a reason why great leaders have consistently high expectations and why struggling organizations have adopted, albeit often unintentionally, more moderate standards of performance.

Ensure Mutual Accountability

Accountability is everyone's responsibility. The most successful teams understand that accountability is not a management activity but a promise that every person makes to give his or her best and to ensure that others do the same.

Learn to Love Different

Diversity of thought, information, and ideas are the foundations of creativity, learning, and change. We are not always conscious of how our beliefs affect our judgment—but we need to be.

Seek Commitment, Not Compliance

We need a different theory of motivation, one likely to gain commitment and not just compliance. Our addiction to a theory of motivation based on the manipulation of rewards and punishments is not only outdated but counterproductive.

Embrace Vulnerability

Effective leadership requires that leaders be willing to act vulnerably. Too often leaders have been rewarded for acting as though they are the smartest people in the room.

You Have to Believe

We have been lucky. We have learned from a diverse group of exemplary leaders who have demonstrated the power inherent in the belief that every person is a source of creative contribution. They provided us with examples of how building engaged teams can create success in the marketplace, on the ball field, in the classroom and in organizations committed to solving some of the world's most pressing social issues.

Their experiences demonstrate that one size does not fit all and that every organization is as unique as the people who work there. Because these leaders understand that they must trust the uniqueness of their 'inner voice,' they spend less time copying others and more time discovering a better way to help their teams create more successful, and more fulfilling futures. They taught us that the biggest impediment to greatness is our own resistance to leaving the comfort of the present. They taught us that the best don't necessarily know more. The best distinguish themselves by summoning the courage to *act* on what they know, by changing themselves before expecting others to change and by attracting others to do the same.

Yet, despite the diversity of their styles, personalities and inner voices, we found that there was one common belief that is universally held by exemplary leaders. They believe in the potential of ordinary people to make extraordinary contributions and they expect them to do the extraordinary routinely. They believe that it is the belief in, and the love for people that make it possible for a team of talented individuals to do what others think can't be done.

What does love have to do with leading great teams? Just about everything.

Choose Love, Not Fear

One evening an old Cherokee told his grandson about a battle that goes on inside people. He said, "My son, the battle is between two wolves inside us all. One is FEAR. It is anger, jealousy, sorrow, greed, and arrogance. The other is LOVE. It is joy, peace, hope, serenity, humility, kindness, and empathy.

The grandson thought about it for a minute and then asked his grandfather, "Which wolf wins?"

The old Cherokee simply replied, "The one that you feed."

– Anonymous

After Clemson won the 2016 NCAA College Football National Championship over Alabama on a last-second touchdown pass, Clemson's coach, Dabo Swinney, surprised many during his on-field interview with ESPN's Sam Ponder when he told her about his talk with Clemson players before the game.

"I told them that the difference in the game was gonna be love," Dabo said. "That has been my word all year. Love. And I said tonight: we're gonna win it because we love each other. I told them at halftime that we're gonna win the game."[1]

Those of us who know William Christopher (Dabo) Swinney were not the least bit surprised by his belief that love played a role in Clemson's win. In fact, to understand the culture of Clemson's football program is to understand that the love these players and coaches have for each other is—in their minds—fundamental to how they recruit, how they practice, and how they play. However obvious it was to Clemson coaches, crediting love for winning a football game turned out to be a bridge too far for some.

In an article the next morning, Tom Jones of the *Tampa Bay Times* told Dabo to "cool it a little."[2] After noting Clemson's amazing record with Swinney at the helm, as well as the coach's commitment to academics and integrity, he questioned the assertion that love was fundamental to the team's success.

"What does love have to do with it?" Jones asked.

Based on our experience, the short answer is *almost everything.* Choosing to lead from love and not fear is perhaps the most important choice that leaders make as they begin to build an effective team culture. Choosing love, and asking others to do the same, is the inescapable first step toward achieving greatness.

This was the lesson we first learned from SAS Group CEO Jan Carlzon nearly 25 years ago after he led SAS from the roadkill of European airlines to the European airline of the year. He told us the first choice every leader needs to make is to choose to lead from love or to choose to lead from fear. He believed the choice was binary, that every time we choose love, we reduce the debilitating effects of fear—to choose one is not to choose the other. Carlzon was convinced that choosing to lead from love is the only rational first choice for a leader hoping to engage people in finding more creative solutions.

He warned us that choosing love is a choice that is easier to talk about than to execute. "Given the choice, love or fear, nearly everyone will tell you that they choose love. But that is not reality. Most leaders are far more addicted to the use of fear than we might like to think." He was right then. Sadly, he would be right now.

No one likes to think that they purposely use fear to get what they want; no one wants to be *that* person. However, the ugly truth is that many of us do choose fear, even if unintentionally. From grades in school, to performance appraisals, to contingent pay schemes, fear is the inevitable byproduct of many of the management practices that we have inherited. The use of fear to control has become so common that we hardly notice the unintended effects of our choices. Because many of us believe that these practices have worked well enough for us in the past, we are often hesitant to change despite knowing that these methods tend to inhibit connection and distract us from achieving our goals.

We can no longer afford to perpetuate fear-inducing practices or tolerate people who do. The waste of human potential that results from relying on fear to control is growing more expensive by the day, and the science that demonstrates the potential benefits inherent in connections based on positive emotion is compelling. When the way we connect says, "I care about you. I have your back. I have your best interests at heart. You are safe here," we invite more positive emotions into our lives. Less connected to fear, people tend to be more open to new information. Learning is accelerated. Creativity is more likely. People are more likely to try new things. Mistakes seem less fatal. When we connect more positively and eliminate unnecessary fear, we are more willing to invite joy, hope, interest, and gratitude into our lives.

Choosing love is not a soft or impractical choice. It is a choice that is consistent with what we know about why people make commitments. No matter the venue, every team is made up of people who need to connect, who thrive on positive emotion, and who can be inhibited by fear and uncertainty. Choosing love is a strategic choice that is just as important in the largest public company as it is in a fourth-grade classroom. It is the not-so-well-kept secret why some teams win more consistently than others.

We can assure you that neither Dabo Swinney nor Jan Carlzon sees choosing love as impractical. They both see it as a choice that makes winning more likely. And, like most great leaders, both love winning. They hate losing. "The fun is in the winning," Dabo likes to say. And to know him is to know that he means it. He loves winning almost as much as he loves people. For him, choosing to build a culture based on love is a non-delegable responsibility that is fundamental to building a winning program.

Love is the Glue of High-Performance Cultures

Tom Jones of the *Tampa Bay Times* clearly was not buying Dabo's argument that love was Clemson's competitive advantage. It was clear that Jones believed that winning football games had less to do with love and more to do with the remarkably talented Clemson football players.

It is hard to argue with his assertion that talent is important. You can't beat Alabama without extraordinary talent. It's no secret that Dabo's success at Clemson is more-than-a-little attributable to the fact that he is among the most compelling recruiters in the country. Spend 10 minutes with him, and you will want to play. Spend 15 minutes with him, and you might even believe you can. That said, talent alone has never been enough to create a truly exceptional team. The world is full of talented teams that continually underperform.

Great leaders understand that teams are not simply collections of talented individuals. You can't add up a team's cumulative IQ or cumulative 40-yard sprint times and know who will win the game. Understanding the individual strengths of team members tells you little about team capabilities, in the same way that understanding hydrogen and oxygen tells you little about the properties of water. Over time, teams develop their own identities as people learn what the team values and what the team doesn't. People on teams learn quickly which actions are acceptable and which are likely to be career-limiting. They learn whether questioning present practices is safe, whether innovation is important, and whether people will be treated with respect. They get the message early on as to whether they can build relationships based on trust or if they should watch their backs.

Only when a team's identity is built on a shared belief that relationships on the team must be based on positive emotion will people feel safe taking risks and finding creative solutions to thorny problems. When people feel satisfied, safe, and emotionally connected, they won't feel the need to spend as much time worrying about their relationships with their bosses or their teachers or their coaches. They will feel accepted and valued. Learning will feel more natural. And, because they trust more and fear less, they will be more likely to see new possibilities and to bounce back more quickly from setbacks.

When you meet teams in which people care deeply about each other, there is an energy that you can feel almost immediately. Call it a "winning spirit" or "competitive spirit," on these teams, the way people relate to each other is different and exhilarating. There is a glue that connects individuals to each other and connects every individual to his or her team's shared sense of purpose. We may not all call that glue 'love,' but on these teams it is positive emotion, not fear, that makes it more likely that people will reach closer to their potential.

Dabo calls the glue the team's culture, the collective character of the team that can make winning more likely. Others may not call it culture. They may say, "It's how we do things here," or "It's our collective habits and beliefs that guide our actions." But no matter what words they choose, the most effective leaders understand that a team's culture goes a long way toward determining success. They understand that choosing to care is an individual choice. But they are ever mindful that great teams are founded on the shared willingness of team members to collectively choose to connect differently. Therefore, the best leaders refuse to leave the development of the team's culture to chance.

When Dabo told Sam Ponder that Clemson was going to beat Alabama because the team members loved each other, we believe that he was saying what—to him—was obvious. He believed that Clemson was going to win because the players were prepared to win. They had developed the collective character, the 'culture' in his words, to execute in the big games; to give people the best chance to play their best when it counts the most. Dabo was not saying that love alone would win football games. We believe that he was saying that the Clemson team had developed a winning spirit based on genuine caring and respect that enabled them to play with less fear and more joy.

Choosing Love is Contagious

Creating a culture in which connections are based on love is something better worked on than achieved. Every culture is a work in progress. It begins with an individual choice to love and grows as that choice is reciprocated. What begins with a small group opting to care for each other can become cultural as more people experience the benefits inherent in more positive connections.

Success will require that we become intentional in the way we spend our time, the stories we tell, and the dialogues we create. It will require that we spend more time looking for the good in others, that we assume the best of intentions on the part of every member of the team, and that we commit to an uncommon level of honesty. These are no small changes for most of us.

The good news is that we—in our roles as both leaders and team members—want to relate more positively. We want to have good relationships with the people on our teams. It's the way we're built. We are social animals. As kids, we can't survive without connection. That need does not diminish as we grow up. We are hardwired to connect. As adults, our need for the emotional nourishment inherent in positive connection is as real as our need for food. It changes us, the way we see the world, and even the chemistry of our bodies. It can provide a pathway to learning and growth. As positive emotions grow, they can reach a tipping point that changes the culture of the team and broadens what the team believes is possible.

Recent scientific research explains why leading from love is contagious. We now know that positive emotion produces a hormone called oxytocin that counteracts the effects of fear-induced stress hormones and can lead not only to better health but also to an increased willingness and ability to collaborate and learn over time.

> *. . . oxytocin is a very unique neurochemical; the more oxytocin we make, the stronger our body and mind respond to it. Our nerve cells actually sprout more oxytocin receptors, making them more sensitive to its effects. It grows easier and easier to be loving. Oxytocin is the neurochemical basis for the adage, 'the more you give, the more you get.' Love tends to breed more love and fear tends to breed more fear. It's up to us.*[3]

Love begets love. Fear begets fear. More love and less fear should not be a controversial choice. It should not even be a difficult one. But the old adage "we should not 'should' on ourselves," seems appropriate. We often don't do what we know to be in our best interest. At times, we are simply not comfortable with what we know we should do. Unfortunately, many leaders still find it difficult to believe that something as "soft" or "fuzzy" as "leading from love" is fundamental to winning football games, increasing earnings, or transforming organizations. Too many still believe that choosing love over fear is an impractical choice that cannot consistently produce results in a world that is increasingly results-oriented.

What does love have to do with building great teams? Honestly, *almost everything* is not an exaggeration.

The Unconscionable Cost of Fear

To put it simply, fear makes us dumber. When we are fearful, we are less coordinated, less connected, and slower to solve problems. Decades of research have shown that fearful environments make us quicker to assign blame, less likely to be collaborative, less likely to be creative, and less likely to learn. Fear incites a primal flight or fight response in us, an internal call to battle stations. It narrows our view of the world and invites us to seek out the protection of the comfortable. Fear motivates us. It motivates us to eliminate the fear.

This isn't always a bad thing. In fact, our primal response to the perception of danger—being fearful of putting our hands on a hot stove, for example—is a good thing. The fear that drives us to lock our doors at night or tell our kids not to talk with strangers makes our lives safer. These evolutionary defensive responses are hardwired in our brains. These responses help us sense potential danger and trigger survival mechanisms that work for our benefit.

Some fear is unavoidable, even natural. When we choose to participate in activities that pose little physical danger but could embarrass or disappoint us, we can feel fearful. Every athlete who chooses to compete, every student who enters a class, every person who applies for a job usually feels some degree of discomfort or fear in the process. This type of fear is an unavoidable consequence of participation.

When we talk about choosing love and not fear, we are not advocating that we try to avoid the unavoidable tension that comes from risking failure through participation or competition. We are advocating that we take a mindful look at the unnecessary fear that we intentionally or unintentionally create to "manage" the performance of individuals and teams. We are suggesting that we question the assumptions that form the foundations of many of our inherited leadership and management practices. When we do, we believe that we will reach the inescapable conclusion that, too often, we have chosen to adopt fear-inducing methods because they are what we know, because they are often easier to implement, and because they provide us with an illusion of control.

As we become more mindful of how our reliance on traditional management practices evoke fear, we can't help but become acutely aware of the high, unconscionable cost we are paying for our unwillingness to choose less fearful practices that make high levels of engagement more likely. According to

Gallup, only about 30% of workforce members are highly engaged in their work.[4] As though that were not problem enough, approximately 17% of people are actively disengaged. That is, they come to work every day acting in ways that purposefully undermine the goals of their organizations. It is nothing short of mind-boggling to think that more than one in six members of our teams are actively working to undermine our efforts.

The trend is not good, despite significant investment. Over the last decade, the number of engaged employees is up only slightly, and the group that is least engaged is millennials, those born between 1980 and the turn of the century.[5] Even more troubling, millennials have become the largest generation in the U.S. workforce and the very people who will be responsible for determining our future.

No wonder 92% of North American respondents to the *Survey of the Global Agenda* said that we are in a leadership crisis today.[6] Eighty-six percent of respondents worldwide agreed. It's a crisis because, at the very time when we need different, better, and more human leadership that engages the hearts and minds of the people on our teams, we are failing. It seems that we're failing primarily because we have not come to grips with the fact that influence is relational and that unleashing the potential of people is about, well, mostly people.

Research done by the Gurnek Bains team at YSC shed significant light on what we feel is the path of our leadership crisis.[7] The global consulting firm studied 1,500 global leaders, revealing their strengths and weaknesses. Their findings reflected what many have suspected for years: today's leaders have similar strengths and weaknesses. They tend to be ambitious, action-oriented, analytical, and commercially minded. The primary weaknesses of today's leaders? They tend to fail on nearly every dimension of human interaction. Only about a quarter of the leaders studied showed significant empathy, self-awareness, insight, and authenticity—all of the human traits necessary to build and maintain the relationships that give them the ability to lead.

Maybe the most damning trend is how quickly leaders are losing trust. According to public relations firm Edelman, less than 25% of professionals trust their leaders to tell the truth when confronted with a difficult issue.[8] When the subject is government, not business, we tend to trust even less. In its 2018 global trust and credibility research, Edelman reported that nearly 70% of the 33,000 participants believed that "building trust is the number one job of CEOs, ahead of high-quality products and services."

These studies can serve as a reality check on our present practices. They highlight the waste of human potential that can result when we let the tyranny of past customs inhibit our ability to find a more effective way to engage and lead in the future. We believe that the power of our collective efforts is only limited by our courage and our imaginations. To maximize the human potential in a world that promises very little predictability and certainty, we must find a way to become more comfortable in the inherent discomfort of innovation and change. We must eliminate practices that rely on fear to control. We must embrace practices that enhance positive connection and provide a level of psychological safety. The people on our teams deserve better.

Is the Feedback Developmental or Fear-Inducing?

A colleague of ours liked to say that feedback is the breakfast of champions. At first blush, his point seemed obvious: it's hard to learn anything without thoughtful and relevant feedback. By borrowing the long-time cereal tagline, he made the importance of feedback memorable. We like the simplicity of the saying. But, as with all simple sayings, the reality is far more complicated. For many people today, feedback can actually serve to increase fear and, therefore, stifle learning and development.

We were recently working with an organization that manufactures medical compounds that support clinical trials. This company is a high-reliability organization that tightly regulates every step in the manufacturing process. Processes are tightly controlled because any failure in production can create systemic delays, add additional costs, or endanger patients who might ingest unsafe medications. Knowing that even a single failure might lead to catastrophic consequences, the company prided itself on having developed a 'quality first' culture. As the organization grew, however, the pressures to efficiently increase production had resulted in a growing number of quality problems. To address the increased quality variability, the company demanded more accountability from its technicians. Management created a process in which two technicians, instead of one, had to sign each batch record at every key step in the process. The thinking was that having a checker check the checker would ensure compliance.

Unsurprisingly, this attempt to increase quality did not work as planned. The heightened pressure to eliminate mistakes, combined with the increased bureaucracy and a threat of greater accountability, did not reduce the number of variations. In fact, the number of mistakes increased and on every indice of quality things got worse. Sadly, but predictably, the frustrated managers blamed the technicians. Believing that the technicians either "didn't care" or were "sloppy," they instituted what they called a "three strikes policy." If a team member was involved in three quality variations, he or she was subject to progressive levels of discipline that could affect his or her career. Management believed that this would get people to be more careful and to pay attention to the details. This 'accountability process,' as it was called, did neither. It did, however, lead to higher levels of fear among the technicians and even more quality issues. The team learned, albeit the hard way, that even in manufacturing suites, fearful people rarely perform at a high level.

The managers who devised the three strikes and the "let's have the checkers check the checkers" quality improvement efforts had the best of intentions. They were trying to protect the company and the health of the patients served by the drugs they were developing. However, the more fear they unintentionally or intentionally created, the worse the situation became. They told us that they didn't intend to create fear to get compliance, but they readily admitted that fear was a predictable consequence of the actions that they voluntarily adopted.

In the year 2019, it's easy to criticize managers who choose to create a process that assumes that having one person looking over the shoulder of another would improve quality. Most would consider such a practice archaic and non-sensible. However, the use of practices that increase fear through the manipulation of rewards or punishments based on performance feedback is still seen as best practice in many organizations. Too often, we don't realize that fear that is created when feedback is "weaponized" in the process of getting better performance.

The three strikes example might seem a little extreme, but the underlying process should be familiar. Think of the car salesperson who all but begs you to give a high mark in an upcoming customer satisfaction survey. In theory, the purpose of these surveys is to get feedback from which people and the dealership can improve. But because any critical feedback can be career threatening to the salesperson, many will provide discounts or other incentives if the customer provides high grades and no critical feedback. What employee wants critical feedback on a performance appraisal if that feedback might negatively impact his or her career? Give students the choice between a tough test that can become the basis for greater learning or an easy quiz, their answers would surprise no one.

People want and need information that can facilitate learning. Feedback can be the breakfast of champions. Or, it can be fear-inducing and career limiting. The difference is not in the information or in the design of the metrics chosen. The difference is in how the information will be used. Will it be used to help develop competencies in a caring, safe, and respectful way? Or will it be used to manipulate behavior in a way that unnecessarily increases fear?

Most of us don't like to think that we induce fear in others as a way of managing performance. However, even when we don't intend to create fear in others, it is often insidiously present as the result of practices that have become so accepted that their efficacy is rarely questioned.

The bottom line: fear makes us dumber. Choosing fear is choosing to enable our teams to underperform. Yet still, we persist.

Lead with Warmth Before Competence

Research published by Amy Cuddy of Northwestern, Susan Fiske of Princeton, and Peter Glick of Lawrence University indicates that when we judge leaders, we initially look at two characteristics: (1) "how lovable they are (their warmth, communion, or trustworthiness) and (2) how fearsome they are (their strength, agency, or competence)." These two traits may account for as much as 90% of how we differentiate one leader from another.[9]

Interestingly, this research indicates that it matters which of these traits is demonstrated first. The evidence is growing that Jan Carlzon had it right when he told us that we must lead with love. It seems that when we focus on our relationships first (lead with warmth and empathy), we are saying through our actions that we care, that we can be trusted, that we are listening, and that we mean people no harm. When people feel safe, they are more open to new ideas and more willing to take risks. The research clearly indicates that people's perception of our warmth contributes far more to their evaluations of us than does their initial perception of our competence.

Unfortunately, the number of leaders who lead with warmth first is a relatively small group. The cultural pressures that lead many to try to demonstrate their competence first must not be underestimated. We want to be seen as strong. We understand that appearing strong and confident and in control is often rewarded. We want to show that we will get the job done. The culture can send an unmistakable message: results matter most.

These all-too-common cultural messages that prod us to lead with competence first can have the effect of undermining our ability to influence. Without trustworthy relationships, people are far less likely to adopt a team's values and mission. Without a common sense of purpose, collaboration often suffers and fear and envy in the organization are more likely to grow. Research by Jack Zenger and Joseph Folkman seems to reinforce the fact that warmth and popularity matter. They found that very few people are both unlikable and highly effective. Only 27 of the 51,836 leaders they studied were rated in the bottom quartile in terms of likability and the top quartile in terms of overall effectiveness.[10]

We have all heard it. You have probably said it yourself: "I would rather be respected than liked. Leadership is not about being liked." It appears that old saying may need some updating. Maybe being liked, being perceived as caring, warm, empathetic, and loving, is more important than we may have thought in the past. Maybe the new wisdom should be that we should strive to be liked and respected. It may be critical to be liked in order to have the opportunity to be highly respected.

Jan Carlzon had it right: love first. Choose to lead first with warmth. Like it or not, it has the greatest effect on how people view you and how willing they will be to trust you. After you have developed a trusting relationship with them, people will be better able to appreciate your strength and competence.

Love 'em Up Before You Coach 'em Up

Alan Mulally is a different type of leader. When you meet him, you quickly note that he is kind, driven, and naturally curious. His interpersonal skills are informed by the type of caring about people that is unmistakably special. From the way that he treats wait staff at restaurants to the way that he makes you feel in conversations, the love that fuels every one of his interactions is palpable. He connects and influences with ease. But make no mistake, the intense, competitiveness of the engineer that worked on every Boeing jet from the 707 to the 777 and rose to become the CEO of Boeing Commercial Airlines is also readily apparent. Within minutes of meeting him, you immediately begin to understand why people want to follow him and why he succeeded in leading one of the most storied turnarounds in business history: the transformation of the Ford Motor Company.

When Alan took the helm at Ford, the company was in trouble. In 2006, the company lost almost $13 billion. Its debt was rated as junk, the company sat on the brink of bankruptcy, and few people on the management team were optimistic that things would get better quickly. However, when he retired from Ford eight years later, the company had been transformed. Profits were at a record high; Ford posted 19 consecutive quarters in the black, and frontline employees were receiving bonuses of nearly $9,000 a year.

Alan is a strong competitor. His commitment to accountability and performance is unmistakable in conversations. These traits were undoubtedly necessary as 'the airline guy' led a historically successful transformation of 'car guys,' all with largely the same management team that he had inherited.

One of the first things that Alan mentioned when talking about his journey at Ford struck us and still guides many of our conversations. He likes to say that, as leaders, you have to "love 'em up before you can coach 'em up." This saying is part of Alan's 'put people first' mentality, and it seems to be his intuitive recognition of the wisdom in the old adage, "People don't care how much you know until they know how much you care." For us, Alan's saying serves as a gentle reminder that how you 'show up' speaks volumes about you and your trustworthiness.

Alan's advice to 'love 'em up' first is similar to the advice offered by both Jan Carlzon and Dabo Swinney. The advice is so simple, so commonsensical, that it should be adopted as a standard practice by any leader who desires to build a great team. Yet, inexplicably, too many leaders underestimate the effect of connection on performance. Too many of us are still too willing to let custom influence our decisions.

Choose love first. Choose to lead with warmth. Like it or not, believe it or not, this choice has a profound effect on how people view you and how willing they will be to trust you. As you start this transformative journey, we encourage you to think about three things that Alan Mulally's mother repeated to him every day, over and over again, like a mantra.

- The purpose of life is to love and be loved, in that order.
- To serve is to live.
- It is nice to be important, but more important to be nice.

Chapter 1 | Summary

1. Choosing love, not fear, is a choice to build a culture based on positive emotion, one that broadens our view of the world and allows us to believe that more things are possible.
2. It is our social connection that provides people with a sense of safety, broadens their horizons, and gives them the power to resist following the herd. Love is more than a positive emotion. It is a lens through which the best leaders view all other choices.
3. Choosing fear makes us dumber. It sends us to battle stations. Fear narrows our world view, impedes learning, and lessens creative expression.
4. Too often we have mindlessly perpetuated fear-inducing practices without a full understanding of the underlying costs of those practices. Many of us are more addicted to using fear to give us an illusion of control than we might like to believe.
5. Choosing love is not a tactic. It is a reflection of who you are, your belief in people, and the confidence you have in yourself. People have great BS detectors. Saying that we care deeply when our actions don't match our words destroys trust and reduces our ability to influence others.
6. It is important that we lead with warmth before we try to prove our competence. All influence is relational. Trying to show our competence first can make us appear manipulative and unlikable. It can undermine trust and, without a trusting relationship, our ability to influence the future is severely limited.

7. Choosing Love is contagious. Each person who chooses to show they care makes it more likely that the next person will do the same.
8. We influence others through the actions we take, the conversations we create and the stories we tell. In choosing love not fear it can bc hclpful to routinely ask:
    a. What more can we do to tell people that we care, that we appreciate who they are and what they have contributed?
    b. What can we do to set a better example of what it means to care deeply about the people on our teams?
    c. What might we stop doing that unintentionally sends a wrong message to members of our team, causing them to doubt our commitment to serving each other?
    d. Who has helped us this week? Who has supported our efforts and made our lives better? How have we thanked them?

Create a Cause Worthy of Commitment

"That business purpose and business mission are so rarely given adequate thought is perhaps the most important cause of business frustration and failure."

– Peter Drucker

"To do some idiotic job very well is certainly not real achievement. I like my phrasing, what is not worth doing is not worth doing well."

– Abraham Maslow

Leadership is change. The best leadership is transformative. It is leading a team from somewhere to somewhere significantly better. It requires engaging with others so they will choose to take responsibility for helping to create a different future. As leaders, it is our responsibility to connect the present to the future, today's reality with what's possible tomorrow, and to do so in a way that engages the heart as well as the mind.

When we ask people to engage with us to create a better future, their response is predictable. Nearly universally, they ask, "Where are we going?" And then, "Why is it important?" They don't initially respond by asking about our leadership style or the details of our plan. They want to know whether our vision of what we hope to create in the future is interesting and worthy of their commitment. They are looking for a reason to get excited, a reason to get passionately engaged.

An effective vision of the future is an invitation, a description of an opportunity that is so compelling that people are moved to action. When leaders prove successful at engaging people in a worthy cause, it's usually because they have described the intended future state:

1. With enough specificity that the team understands what is intended;
2. In a way that is emotionally engaging, that, if achieved, people will be able to find significant meaning in their efforts; and
3. In a way that tells the team, through their words and actions, that they are passionately and unambiguously committed.

Despite every leadership book, theory, and guru evangelizing the importance of a shared vision for the future, we have found that most leaders and their teams do not share a common view of their intended destinations. The many mind-numbing vision meetings that we have attended have done little to create compelling visions. Do a Google search and you'll find more than 105 million entries that discuss the importance of a shared vision. Sadly, despite this library of advice, most attempts to create a compelling, shared understanding of the future have not resulted in a narrative that invites engagement and creativity. More often, these attempts at "vision sharing" have resulted in team frustration and a tacit understanding among team members that the future will look a lot like yesterday.

0 for 65: You Can't Create What You Haven't Envisioned

Several years ago, the CEO of a market-leading, mid-sized company told us that he was frustrated with his inability to create a culture that supported higher levels of creativity and innovation. He believed that innovation was critical to the company's future success, but he sensed that few people shared his sense of urgency. He wanted to shake things up. He believed strongly that a culture of innovation meant that every person must become a source of creative thought. He wanted to see transformation in the organization's culture even as it celebrated another year as the market leader in its industry.

The CEO called for a vision meeting. He believed that people needed a more inspiring view of the future. However, his personal distaste for vision meetings was no secret. He didn't even like the word vision—the "V-word" as he liked to call it. "One of the most overused words on the planet," he would say. But he knew people would not help create what they had not envisioned, so he decided to kick off the process with an all-hands meeting. He wanted to get people fired up about what they could accomplish in the future.

The meeting was fun. The music rocked. The CEO's talk was inspiring and people appeared to be excited. Employees cheered when he asked each of them to "reach deep, dream big, and find a way to be different tomorrow." They cheered even louder when he described his own commitment to personal development. He went on to explain how the entire team would benefit from the growth that would ensue as their innovations changed the trajectory of the market.

The standing ovation the CEO received was genuine. His message resonated with the group. They were, as several people later told us, eager to take responsibility for doing something "remarkable."

Understanding that the momentum of the rally would not last forever, the CEO knew that he needed to create a structure to ensure that the team maintained a steady focus on innovation. He decided to send an email to each of the top 65 leaders in the company asking them to articulate a vision for their groups that would require their groups to innovate faster. He asked each member of this extended leadership team to answer the following questions:

1. What is your vision for your team 18-24 months from now?
2. How is that substantially different from your team's performance today?
3. Why are these changes critical for our organization?
4. How are you going to personally change to ensure the effort is successful?

When the CEO received their responses, he was frustrated. Not a single one of the 65 leaders had provided a clear description of what they intended to create in the future. For most, their description of the future could best be described as, "just like today, only a little better."

Describing the situation to us, the CEO grew even more frustrated. "No wonder we are not changing, we have not described a future worthy of their sacrifice. People are not excited about our future. We have a dearth of imagination among members of our leadership team, and it's killing us. It's unrealistic to expect people to get excited about the prospect of working hard to accomplish what they have already accomplished."

As he continued to think about the responses he had received, it occurred to him that *his* description of the future of the company was far from awe-inspiring. For all his distaste for the vision word and his belief that the word was overused, he had not provided a vision of the company's future that would lead people to sacrifice for the collective good. He realized that the team had no role model, no good example whom the team could look to as a "North Star" to guide their efforts. He felt silly. He had kicked off this effort to bring excitement to what comes next before he had created a vision of what comes next. "It's hard to create or get excited about something that you have not envisioned," he told us.

This leader's experience in "non-vision setting" is more the rule than the exception. After more than a decade of asking leaders to describe a clear and compelling vision of the future, we have found that, absent a crisis, leaders rarely communicate visions that are clear and compelling. Most have defaulted to a process that attempts to be slightly better than they were last year. The unintended effect of these "more of the same" non-visions is that they rob the team of the energy required to change, innovate, and achieve remarkable results.

Meaning Can Turn a Vision into a Cause

When visions are compelling, they connect people with possibility and move them to action. Effective visions are not simply clear descriptions of a future state; they are emotional pleas to get involved. They are invitations to participate in something important. They are more akin to joining a cause than simply sharing a vision. Causes provide the real possibility that participation will allow us to find meaning in our actions. And when we find meaning, our actions take on a more human quality. Where we find meaning, we tend to find more love, kindness, empathy, understanding, respect, and courtesy. In meaning-filled cultures, we are better able to express our humanity, to transcend the mundane, and to become part of something bigger than ourselves.

Meaning matters more than we realize. It is a primary driver of our actions and our commitments. In study after study over the last couple of decades, researchers have confirmed that people who feel a strong sense of purpose in their efforts are three times more likely to be engaged. These studies simply confirm what Viktor Frankl, the world-renowned psychiatrist and author of *Man's Search for Meaning*, taught us a half a century ago: it is that only when we find profound meaning in our actions will we be willing to make significant commitments, find true fulfillment in our efforts, and connect with people we hope might join us.[1]

Our search for meaning is uniquely human. It is one of the things that separates us from other life forms. Our search can be messy and time-consuming and often requires imagination, dialogue and empathy. But, it is our search for meaning and purpose that moves us to transcend the pettiness of everyday life, to sacrifice our personal needs for the greater good, and to find fulfillment in service to others. It is our drive to find meaning that turns a vision into a cause worthy of our commitment.

In our quest to articulate a cause that is so compelling that people will readily enlist, it is important to remember that meaning cannot be given. It can only be found. The search for meaning is personal; meaning is a matter of the heart and the mind. One person's personal crusade can be uninteresting to others. As leaders, the best we can hope to do is to create environments where as many people as possible can find meaning in their collective actions. In most cases, finding meaning is the result of a reflective process and dialogue. It is almost never the result of buying into someone else's vision. It is almost always the result of a collective commitment to pursue an opportunity where team members feel that they can make a significant difference in the lives of others.

When people ask "Where are we going?" and "Why is it important?" they are asking us to help them find a reason to make a commitment. They are looking for a cause in which they can find meaning that will enrich their lives. People were born to find meaning. They want to take responsibility for serving others and for doing something remarkable. Connecting people to a cause in which meaning can be found is a leader's primary responsibility.

Aren't There Jobs Where Meaning is Difficult to Find?

The short answer to this question is yes. There are jobs in which meaning is difficult to find—in some cases, even impossible to find. However, in most cases, it is not the tasks themselves that are devoid of meaning. More often, it is the way the tasks are designed and the way the team is led that make it difficult to find meaning.

Obviously, finding meaning in every endeavor is not as easy as it is when we undertake volunteer activities such as building homes for the homeless. But there is meaning to be found in most activities when the people involved have the opportunity to make significant, mindful, and creative contributions. This is especially true when they are challenged to serve others.

How can someone find excitement or engagement in the cleaning of rooms and scrubbing of toilets?

If that is all the job entails, it's a tough lift to think that people will become passionate about cleaning toilets. Scrubbing toilets probably should not be the task that defines one's work life. That is the belief of Chip Conley, founder and former CEO of the Joie de Vivre Hotel Group. Based in San Francisco, Joie de Vivre was the second-largest boutique hotel operator in the United States before selling to Marriott. Chip is an avid student of Abe Maslow, the founder of humanistic psychology.

He shares Maslow's belief that people were born with a need to learn, grow, and commit themselves to a greater cause. Although Chip has not been CEO for most of the last decade, his beliefs about the potential of people live on in the culture of many of the company's properties.

Conley's passionate and unwavering belief that all people have the capacity to do extraordinary work caused him to rethink many of the job responsibilities in his hotels. He refused to narrowly define roles in ways that limited expectations of how people should think and act. He believed that every person should make a creative contribution to the mission of the hotel, whether they worked at the front desk or in housekeeping or in engineering.

His beliefs may have been most apparent in the way that he thought about housekeeping. He believed that people working in housekeeping had the potential to do more than clean and refresh rooms. He refused to see the housekeeping staff as just room cleaners. Instead, he reinvented the job and made these team-members 'customer service representatives.' He valued their ideas. Their contributions to guest services were routinely celebrated. Yes, they still cleaned rooms while they looked for guests to serve. But, because the team members roamed the halls of the hotel every day interacting with guests, over time they became an integral part of the service strategy of the hotel and helped the chain build an enviable reputation. Joie de Vivre often had a waiting list for people applying for jobs on its 'housekeeping' teams while most hotels had trouble filling vacancies.

The changes that were made in these hotels went far beyond revising job descriptions. Conley was a true believer in the need for people to find meaning in their work. He believed in the willingness and ability of ordinary people to do remarkable things. His intention was not simply to reinvent housekeeping, but to improve guest service and to enrich the lives of people on the team. It was not a tactic. It was more a reflection of his belief that, in order for his hotels to provide an exemplary guest experience, employees must first be engaged.

"I give out parking tickets. That's my job!" That's what a university parking enforcement professional once told us. She told us that on most days her job was monotonous and unfulfilling. She thought that she was probably the most disliked person on campus. "Who likes to be the person who puts the ticket on your windshield? People look the other way when they see me coming," she explained.

After talking with her for 10 minutes, it was easy for us to understand why parking enforcement officers are not always passionately engaged. They often work alone. They don't make people happy. The job doesn't challenge them intellectually. The responsibilities are repetitive. Find the offender. Write the ticket. After talking with her, we understood why she felt that some days seemed a month long.

We are pretty sure that there are no rules that state that the sole job of a parking enforcement officer is enforcing parking regulations. Just as was the case with hotel housekeepers, there must be a better way to design the job that would both add more value to students and allow the 'parking professional' a better chance to find meaning.

Would the job be more engaging if the 'parking officer' were a 'student safety officer' who roamed the campus looking for students to help? The question seems almost rhetorical. With all of the problems faced by students today, having roving assistance officers would likely increase the perception of safety on campuses while at the same time increasing the satisfaction of the officers, who would have the opportunity to serve students in need. Yes, enforcing parking regulations would still be part of the job. However, it would no longer be the only focus of the job.

What are we waiting for? If simple changes in job design can enrich the lives of our hard-working, committed teammates, it seems silly to perpetuate jobs that were clearly not designed with people's job satisfaction in mind. Instead of writing another disengaging job description, let's commit to the reinvention of every rote, repetitive job to ensure that people have a realistic chance to find meaning in their efforts.

We still carry with us the words of an employee at a resort in Atlantic City when she answered a question posed by the CEO of a hotel and casino operation. It was an answer that none of us were expecting to hear, and her words ring in our ears every time we see a job that needlessly underestimates the willingness and ability of people to contribute. On that cloudy New Jersey morning, the CEO asked a group of employees what he could do differently to support their efforts. A middle-aged employee looked the CEO in the eye and said, "You can stop treating me like I am not very smart. I may 'make change' in your casino for a living, but that is not all I do. I have raised three generations of kids on my salary. I manage a complicated household. I have sent children to college and made ends meet. And then I come to work and you treat me like I can't think. If you really want to support me, listen to me. I have ideas. I am capable."

Her name was Jennifer. Her message said it all.

To Find Meaning: Evaluate Job Design and Job Performance

In his 1965 book *Eupsychian Management*, Abe Maslow recounted his frustration with narrow job descriptions. After spending a couple of months with Kaypro Computer in San Diego, Maslow was critical of management that expected high levels of motivation despite the fact that many roles were designed so that learning was neither necessary nor supported. Maslow wrote that he "used to think real achievement was possible. But, now I am sure that any job not worth doing is not worth doing well."[2] He was rightfully skeptical that managers could emotionally engage people in doing mindless work or working in an "average chewing gum factory." It was apparent to him that many jobs were designed to be mindless and management often valued obedience more than reasoned decision-making. He believed that these types of jobs robbed people of the opportunity to learn, grow, and achieve. He believed that these jobs sapped people of their natural desire to make a meaningful difference.

We are not sure that Maslow would be any happier with many current job designs. Today, it is not just housekeepers and parking officers whose job descriptions inhibit engagement and make it difficult for people to find meaning in their efforts. In many call centers, people still need a supervisor's approval before making simple decisions. Too often, school teachers' methods are unnecessarily restricted and retail clerks cannot approve simple returns. Maslow's assertion half a century ago continues to ring true: we can't separate people's engagement from what they are being asked to do. We can't expect to capture the creative contributions of people if we continue to systematically underestimate their abilities. It's lunacy to expect people to get excited about tasks that we know are unexciting.

We suggest that we become more mindful of a job's potential to engage the hearts and minds of people. We suggest that at least annually we evaluate job design as well as job performance. We should ask:

1. How well is the job being done? (Performance)
2. Is the job designed in such a way that job holders can find meaning worthy of their sacrifice? (Job design)
3. Is the job design unnecessarily limiting?
4. How might we broaden job responsibilities to further challenge people to make a larger contribution?

This advice comes with a warning label: Beware of those who might suggest shortcuts in the process of redesigning responsibilities. Any attempt to redefine a job begins in the heart of the leader. Only when we believe, really believe, in the ability of people to make greater contributions are we likely to redefine work in meaningful ways. We must assume that people are smart and are willing to take more responsibility. We must keep in mind that the only jobs in which people will be proud of making a contribution are those in which people already are making a contribution. Calling a job challenging or meaningful or professional doesn't make it so.

Many of the leadership books written in the last few decades include a story of a bricklayer who was more committed to his job because he believed that he was building a cathedral, not just laying bricks. This story is often told to demonstrate the power of meaning and contribution.

Conceptually, the "bricks are part of a cathedral" example makes sense. It is hard to disagree with the notion that we can find more meaning in our work when we feel part of the greater mission of an organization. However, what worries us is how often leaders have taken this story and used it to attempt to create a shortcut to employee engagement by deciphering the lesson of the story in an oversimplified way.

Merely telling bricklayers that they are building a cathedral will not result in a transformation in the way they see their work. People know whether the responsibility is real. They can sort out our real motives in seconds. Telling someone that a crappy job is not crappy because it is a part of something bigger is a flawed strategy. People know when they are trusted and valued members of a team. They can feel when they are able to give their best efforts. Changing a job title has a short-lived effect if there is no substance to the change. Trying to get people to feel involved when they are not meaningfully involved only makes us look silly.

I Am the Team: Developing a Shared Commitment

Developing a shared sense of purpose, a commitment to a cause that stirs people to action, takes on many forms. It helps when the leader of the team can articulate a description of the future state in a way that excites the team. But even when the leader is captivating, creating a shared sense of purpose usually requires substantial dialogue and debate. It takes time. It often requires patience as team members work to make the decision to commit. However, when a team is successful, the level of commitment that results can be surprising and energizing. The power inherent in a shared cause should not be underestimated.

"I am... Gymboree"

Gymboree, the mall-based children's clothing chain, had fallen on tough times. The late Stuart Moldaw, Gymboree board member and founder of the retailer Ross, set out to recruit Lisa Harper to become CEO. He was sure that Harper, the original clothing designer for Gymboree, was just the person to return the company to its roots: producing high-quality clothes that make children look like, well, children.

As she began what would turn out to be an amazing turnaround story, Lisa selected one of the youngest, most talented teams in retail. They were committed, innovative, fearless, and, like their leader, unconventionally brilliant. On one occasion, we were taken aback when each member of the management team was asked to say, "I am Gymboree." As members of the management team took turns proclaiming that they were Gymboree, we confess that we found the meeting a little, well, cult-like.

When we asked Harper why she wanted her team to say, "I am," she quickly pointed out how different it is for someone to say, "I AM the company," instead of "I work for the company." Her point was that for the turnaround to be successful, the management team would have to make a commitment that wasn't typical. It couldn't be just a job; it had to be more. She believed the team had to make a commitment to be different in the future and had to lead others to do the same. She thought that saying "I AM Gymboree" could be the start of a movement and she hoped that such a movement would infect the rest of the company.

We were skeptical. When we questioned her about the "I AM" statements, she laughed and told us that we didn't quite get it. But with time, she thought we might.

We learned rather quickly that you doubt Lisa Harper at your own risk. We vividly remember attending the first national meeting for top store managers. No matter who we asked or in what setting we posed the question, "How long have you worked for Gymboree?" The answer was the same: "I don't work for Gymboree. I AM Gymboree!"

Each time, we'd laugh. We would remind the employee that Gymboree is a store. A person couldn't be Gymboree. Time and time again, we would hear the same thing: "You don't get it."

Over time, we got used to it. Every year, every store manager, the same story. Lisa had led the company from the brink of disaster to become one of the most successful specialty retailers in the country while building a culture that was fun, engaging, and successful. "I AM Gymboree" had become a way of expressing pride in what the team had created and in what it intended to do in the future. Lisa's method of creating a shared sense of commitment had worked for the Gymboree team.

We were skeptical that Lisa's experience could be generalized until one day we talked with the management group of ESPN shortly after its 25th anniversary. One member pulled out a hat from the celebration. The logo on the hat was "I am ESPN." The ESPN team was quick to point out that Harper had been right years earlier when she told us that when you are part of a team that shares your purpose and values, it is personal. Saying 'I am the company' is just a way of saying 'I am committed.' The company's values are our values. We are all in. Others may do it differently, but the goal is the same. We can't gain commitment to a different future until people passionately believe that the purpose is personal.

Take the Quiz that You Cannot Fail

Dialogues that are effective in gaining shared commitment must answer four questions. We call these four questions the "Quiz That You Cannot Fail." It is adapted from inquiries first suggested by Michigan State professor emeritus and author Karl Frost.[3] He used a version of this quiz to evaluate the readiness of an organization to change. Frost believed that people ask these questions every time they are presented with an opportunity. They may not verbally articulate each question, but they are inevitably seeking answers to all four of these questions before they are willing to fully engage. It is the quiz you cannot fail because failure to address these issues directly and competently increases resistance to change and makes gaining a shared commitment far more difficult.

1. Do we share a vision of where we are going?
   Is that vision clear enough that we can picture the end-state and tell when we have arrived?
2. Why are we going there?
   Do we share a sense of purpose? Do we understand WHY this journey is worthy of our commitment? Can we find meaning in this effort?
3. Are we confident that we can achieve what we have envisioned?
   Do we believe that this team and this leadership are capable and committed to doing whatever is necessary to be successful?
4. Is there enough in this effort for me personally to justify the sacrifices that I will have to make?
   Will I be better off if I commit to the effort?

We are not arguing that addressing these four issues is the magic bullet that will overcome all resistance to change any more than we would argue that saying "I am" the company necessarily leads to a shared commitment. In most cases, people are more wedded to the status quo more than they would like to admit. People love stability and certainty. The anxiety they feel when they are asked to change must not be underestimated.

We are arguing that success is far more likely when leaders are clear in their intent, provide an opportunity where people can find meaning in service to others, have confidence that the team will persist, and instill an understanding among team members about how they will benefit from their sacrifice. We are advocating that these questions become the foundation of an ongoing dialogue within the organization and that team members be encouraged to ask these questions in search of common ground. When individuals feel these issues have been addressed, resistance to change is reduced and the chances of people choosing to engage in creating the future grow exponentially.

Start with Your Description of the Future State

We have found it most effective to start this process by describing the desired future you would like to see for your company, team, or group, then comparing that with present performance. It is only when we are clear in our intent and passionately committed to becoming substantially different from what we are today that we will be willing to make the types of changes that will be required to transform team performance. We have found that most leaders find it difficult to craft a compelling, emotionally engaging description of what they hope to create in the future. This is understandable. It is a skill that has not been honed by most. But if we are passionate about our purpose and clear in our intent, we can improve quickly.

As you start to explore this process, we encourage you to start by asking:

1. What are we, as a team, trying to create in the next 12 to 18 months?
2. How does that compare with present performance?
3. Is the difference significant enough and important enough for people to find meaning in their efforts and to fully engage in the effort?

Think about the following examples and the details included in each one. How are they different? Which do you prefer? Why? We hope that these examples help you in thinking about the type of communications that you might use to kick off a discussion with your team.

Example 1

VERSION 1: We aspire to be the best collegiate athletic department in the country. We want to win games and championships while developing student-athletes and contributing to the overall mission of the university.

ALTERNATIVE: We want to win championships the right way. We want to be known for our sportsmanship. We want every player to develop toward their potential on the field. In addition, we want to help create leaders who will make significant contributions to the university community during their tenure here, while preparing to generate significant contributions to society in the future. We are committed to our core values of honesty, respect, service, and excellence. Both students and staff are role models and, as such, are responsible for ensuring that we are accountable to each other to make our university a better place for all. Each of us is committed to making our university and our athletic programs better today and to helping to create a culture that will help those who come after us.

Example 2

VERSION 1: We aspire to be the best early-stage formulation and manufacturing company in the world.

ALTERNATIVE: We are committed to providing our customers with a unique experience. We provide formulation and manufacturing solutions to our clients in ways that reduce their risks in the process. We are reliable and we understand that quality comes before all other goals. We are flexible. We recognize that nearly every case is a case of first impression (because most every drug we make has never been made before). We embrace the unforeseen, working to ensure that the challenges we face do not negatively impact our clients. We over-communicate, keeping clients informed at every step in the process, and we are honest in our assessment of any challenges we face. We are not wedded to a given technology or solution. We strive to provide our clients with options and to help them select the best solutions based on their individual needs.

Is This a Place Where People Can Find Meaning?

The late Max De Pree, a CEO of the Herman Miller office furniture company and 1992 inductee to the Business Hall of Fame, suggested a line of questions that can help us think about whether people are likely to be engaged in the opportunities they are afforded.[4] Before we communicate our cause and try to engage others in the process, most of us would benefit from considering Max's questions first. Doing so would help us determine whether our vision and our culture are likely to engage the hearts and minds of the people on our teams. What follows is our adaptation of De Pree's questions. No list is complete, so make your own list. Add your own questions. What is important is that you have a framework that comports with what you believe about people and why they choose to go ALL IN in some endeavors and pass on others.

- Am I interested?
- Can I make a difference in the lives of others?
- Is what I do important?

- Am I proud to tell my family and friends that this is what I am doing?
- Are my contributions valued?
- Can I make a difference here?
- Is this a place where I can learn?
- Can I influence the decisions that are made?
- Is this a place where I can reach my potential?
- Do people here care about each other?
- Do we share the same values?

Chapter 2 | Summary

1. Leadership is engaging a team to go from somewhere to somewhere better. If you can't describe where you are going in a clear and compelling way, chances are the team will never get there. The best descriptions of the future are described:
    a. With enough specificity that the team understands what is intended;
    b. In a way that is emotionally engaging and, that if achieved, will enable people to find significant meaning in their efforts; and
    c. In a way that tells the team, through their words and actions, that they are passionately and unambiguously committed.
2. When visions are compelling, they resemble a cause. They provide an opportunity for people to find meaning. They connect people with possibility and move them to action.
3. Many roles have been so narrowly defined that the task becomes rote and repetitive and provides little opportunity for growth. Most of these jobs can be redefined in ways that make engagement more possible and learning more necessary.
4. It should be HR policy to evaluate job design and job performance routinely. Evaluating a person's performance at a mind-numbing job tells you little about that person's potential to make a significant contribution.
5. We should routinely ask people to take the Quiz You Cannot Fail. We need to ensure that people feel that:

a. They share an understanding of what the team is trying to accomplish;
b. The challenge is compelling and worthy of their sacrifice;
c. They are confident in the team's ability to be successful;
d. They will be personally better off if they choose to fully commit to the mission.

Get the Right People On the Team and the Wrong People Off

"The first method for estimating the intelligence of a ruler is to look at the men he has around him."

- Machiavelli

I learned most of what I know about leadership as a soccer player at Santa Clara University."

That is what former Front Range CEO Mike McCloskey told us when we asked him to describe his leadership philosophy. Mike was one of those leaders you just wanted to follow. Humble. Decisive. Curious. Caring. Beneath his soft-spoken manner and smile was an extraordinary competitor. He joined several companies before they had revenue and led them, as CEO, to more than billion-dollar valuations. But, even more impressive than the results of the companies he led was his ability to engage with people. When Mike was about to embark on a new venture, we marveled as members of his past teams called him hoping to enlist.

Working with Mike was always exciting and challenging. He is tough. He is decisive. He expected the best and wanted you to be your best. The lessons we learned in the years we worked with him still resonate:

- Every leader gets to choose only one person who needs serious development.
- Make every customer a reference account.
- Don't let people kiss your ass. You might need to know the truth one day and you need to be able to trust what they are telling you.

Perhaps the lesson that affected us most was the most obvious one: "You have to ensure that you have the right people on the team and you have to ask the wrong people to leave," he told us. As we worked with him, his advice went much further than quoting *Good to Great* author Jim Collins' memorable advice to get the right people 'on the bus.'[1] For McCloskey, ensuring he had the right team was a personal, non-negotiable responsibility. He knew that trying to get the wrong people to do the right things rarely works. He knew that no amount of good leadership is likely to turn a group of the wrong players into a team of champions.

Of the many lessons we learned in our time with McCloskey, patience and discipline in the recruiting process still guide our thinking. Finding the right person for the team was not a new concept for us, but Mike dug deeper, questioned more, and was more cautious. We couldn't understand why it took him so long to hire his team when he made most other decisions at warp speed. We would interview a person who we believed to be a stellar candidate. "This is the one," we would say, only to have Mike hesitate, trust his intuition, and keep looking for the right person.

The best leaders we have met are like Mike. They would rather leave a position vacant than compromise. The best leaders are willing to personally invest time in the hiring process. They enjoy the process. They make it a priority. They involve more people. They want applicants to understand the culture. They don't wait for people to come to them; they go find and recruit the best.

Sure, we all say we *want* to hire the best people. Yet, for all the lip service given to the importance of the hiring process, a disciplined, effective hiring process remains rare. Too often, the discipline required to recruit the right players falls victim to the need to move quickly and get something done. When our need for speed gets us to take short cuts or compromise, we pay a high price for our impatience.

We have to find better ways of getting the right people on the bus. We can no longer afford to use hiring processes that are dependent on divining an applicant's fit from a puffed-up resume. Nor can we afford to waste opportunities by having unprepared people interview candidates or by having search professionals screen applicants without a thorough understanding of the culture of the organization and the role of the potential candidate. Experience in a similar job? Yes, we need to ensure that people have the right competencies to be successful. But three to five to ten years' experience solving yesterday's problems tells us very little about a person's ability to solve tomorrow's challenges.

Invite the Wrong People Off the Team

As hard as it is to find and recruit the best players, for many leaders, it's arguably an even tougher task to get the wrong people off the team—and to do so in a timely manner. For several years, we interviewed leaders who had successfully managed transitions. We asked them what they would do differently if they had a mulligan. Much of what we learned was predictably context-specific. But the one universal response was that they would not tolerate people—especially on the leadership team—who weren't passionately committed to what the group was trying to accomplish. They would move more quickly to get them off the team. One of our clients put the challenge into perspective:

> *We all want people to succeed. We want to give them a chance to develop and change. But when you are leading transitions, and it seems that's all we do today, I would be much quicker to change the team if the leaders involved*

were not fully committed. If it is an ability issue, I would try to help. But if the issue is a willingness to commit, I would have less patience. I spent far too much time trying to convince some members of my team to 'get on board.' Often, they said they were all-in or giving their best, but I knew they were resisting. I thought I could change them. All I did was waste a couple of years. It wasn't fair to the team. People deserve leaders and teammates that are ready to play.

Bruce Nordstrom told us years ago, that the secret to his company's success was ensuring that the best people were there to serve customers every day. The more we talked, the more we were convinced that he had a good idea of the kind of person it took to thrive in that culture.

Nordstrom told us that people need to have skills but that skills are not enough. He was adamant that to be successful, people need to share the organization's values and have a passion for serving. He told us that "working at Nordstrom was not for everyone." Not everyone, he said, "can thrive in a competitive, sales-driven, service-focused culture." and that one of the secrets to the Nordstrom culture was a willingness to part ways with people who didn't share the company's values. At the time, we asked him if it was true that half of the company's employee turnover was the result of letting associates go who didn't fit the culture. His response: "The percentage might be higher." We were surprised until one person in a Northern California store told us that, "It feels good to work for a company that stands for something and where people who are not committed are not allowed to remain part of the team."

Be Clear about Who You Want On the Team

Getting the right people on the team begins with a good understanding of what you intend to accomplish and how you intend to get there. Having clarity as to the game they are playing allows the best leaders to develop more specific profiles of the kinds of people that will be necessary to be successful and gives them a leg up in the recruiting process.

On most great teams, the right people are not always the most talented. Though they have the requisite talents, they are a better fit for other reasons. There are times, though, when we can't quite put our finger on why we feel that one person fits better than another. Yet, after spending time with better leaders, we are convinced that *the more clarity we get, the better our intuition will become.*

At a minimum, leaders who are recruiting for their teams should look for real-life examples that provide evidence that a prospective team member:

- Is interested in, and excited about, what we intend to accomplish,
- Has the requisite skills to succeed in the role,
- Is curious and willing to learn,
- Shares our values,

- Cares for people and is willing to serve others on the team,
- Is self-motivated,
- Will add to the diversity of our team, and
- Is self-confident and willing to speak truth to power.

This is not intended to be a complete list of qualities to consider. It is a starting point. Every team must create its own profile that highlights the characteristics of the "right players," and it must build a process that increases its ability to select people who will not only contribute to, but also enhance its efforts. It is our passion for what we intend to create and our clarity of how we intend to proceed that will reveal the people that we need "on our bus."

Become Less Tolerant of Bad Leaders

Bad leaders are never the right people to have on the team. Those of us who have been on teams led by bad or ineffective leaders can tell you from experience that bad leadership leads to many dark days. Frustrating. Disengaging. Maddening. Every day working for a terrible leader can seem a month long. People deserve better.

Yet, in nearly every organization, bad leaders have been allowed to hang on. In many cases, we have even promoted them, citing their technical competence or that they "made their number" or have a winning record or good test scores. It's time for this to stop. We look silly when we preach a gospel of higher engagement and then accept, tolerate, and promote bad leaders who consistently undermine the very engagement that we spend time and treasure to develop.

Recently, we asked the CEO of a mid-sized company whether she believed that those reporting directly to her were effective leaders. She told us that she knew that most of them "were not good with people." However, she added, "They are good brand ambassadors and big customers like them. I can't afford to lose them. What would happen to the business?"

Even as she told us how the historically positive culture of the organization was being undermined by these ineffective leaders, she could not bring herself to confront them. Really? Why? Why can it be so difficult for so many leaders to confront disrespectful behavior? Why can't we stop acting as accomplices in the demotivation wrought by bad leaders?

Bad leaders are not hard to identify. Robert Sutton, author of the *No-Asshole Rule*, suggests that bad leaders stand out for a variety of reasons. They tend to lob personal insults, invade our personal space, threaten, intimidate, tease inappropriately, humiliate, act rudely, and treat those of lesser status as nearly invisible.[2] If that sounds bad, it's because it *is* bad.

Bad leaders are the worst-kept secret in most organizations, which is why it is so damning for us to look the other way. When we tolerate bad leaders, we are teaching people that bad leadership is acceptable. Worse, we may be demonstrating that over-control, intimidation, shaming, and temper tantrums are permissible. Why do we tolerate this? We look foolish when we say that we are serious about engagement, creativity, and culture development, and then turn around in the next breath and support, even tacitly, bad leaders.

Foolishness aside, it is just the wrong thing to do. And we know it. When we tolerate it for too long, the problems inherent in poor leadership can become entrenched in the culture. When that happens, we can suffer from a 'motivated blindness' in which we lose perspective and begin to underestimate how much we are paying for our unwillingness to act. In a poll of 800 employees and managers spanning 17 industries who had been on the receiving end of a bad leader's incivility, Professors Christine Porath and Christine Pearson found that:

- 48% intentionally decreased their work effort.
- 47% intentionally decreased the time spent at work.
- 38% intentionally decreased the quality of their work.
- 78% said that their commitment to the organization had declined.
- 25% admitted taking their frustrations out on customers.[3]

It's more than a little crazy that we spend so much time and energy trying to create better teams while, at the same time, allowing poor leaders, poor teachers, and abusive coaches to contaminate the very cultures that we are trying to improve. We need to stop the insanity.

Chapter 3 | Summary

1. Ensuring that the right people are on the team facilitates effective leadership, making it more satisfying and more enjoyable. The right people are eager to engage, eager to learn, and eager to make a contribution. They don't need to be jump-started into action. They are, in most cases, self-motivated and eager to be part of something remarkable.
2. Understanding the characteristics of the 'right people' takes time and reflection. Although team needs differ, experience and skills are rarely enough in a world that is changing rapidly. Increasingly necessary are the ability to solve problems that lack obvious answers, the willingness to learn, the confidence to challenge existing norms, and the ability to build relationships with diverse populations.
3. It takes only a few of the 'wrong people' on a team to make building a culture that supports engagement nearly impossible. Many leaders spend too many hours trying to motivate people who have no interest in fully engaging with their teams. The wrong people make great leadership nearly impossible.
4. People deserve good, empathetic leadership. Tolerating bad leadership has become the norm in far too many workplaces. "They are technically outstanding" is not a good reason to allow bad leaders to continue to frustrate the very people whom they are responsible for engaging. Tolerating bad leaders tells the world that bad leadership is acceptable.

5. Finding the right people for the team cannot be rushed. It can be a slow process. Great teams would rather go without a hire for a time than give an offer to the wrong person. Great cultures are great, at least in part, because the best teams take their time in hiring to get the people most likely to help the team succeed.

Dare to Expect Remarkable

"If you can dream it, you can do it."

– Walt Disney

"Whether you believe you can, or you can't, you're right."

– Henry Ford

Walt Disney and Henry Ford had it exactly right. Our performance is—to a large extent—dependent on our beliefs about who we are and who we are not. When we believe that we are smart, we tend to become smarter. If we learn early in life that we have athletic talent, we tend to become better players. When people tell us that we have musical talent, we are more likely to become musicians. Our environments affect our beliefs. Our beliefs can become self-fulfilling. Our beliefs can become ceilings that limit what we believe we can accomplish. This is the way the world works, right up until it doesn't.

For some of us, something happened on the way to having our beliefs become self-fulfilling. Somewhere along the way, we met someone who showed us that we were capable of much more. They believed in our potential and they wasted no time telling us so. They treated us like we were talented. They demanded that we raise our games, and they celebrated with us when we were successful. They taught us that, with support and encouragement, ordinary people could learn to achieve what might not have seemed possible yesterday. Subsequently, people who believed that they could not speak in public learned that they could. The team that didn't believe it could win a league championship started to play like a champion. Over time, people have learned that everything from their IQs to their musical talents can improve with practice. They have learned that there is a better player, a better student inside, just waiting to develop.

High expectations are the not-so-well-kept secret of great teams and great leaders. The best leaders refuse to believe that talents are fixed. Like Henry Ford and Walt Disney, they remind us continually that our potential is unlimited. They believe that ordinary people with confident leadership and a supportive environment can build a car, create a theme park empire, and put a man on the moon. This is not pie-in-the-sky stuff. It's reality; the best leaders won't let us forget that we have far more potential than we have developed to date. The best leaders believe that it is their responsibility to create environments where people feel that they are *stars in waiting.* They create environments where people are willing to consistently test their limits. As one of our colleagues likes to say, we are all born with a Picasso inside us, but somehow along the way, we began to doubt our abilities. The best leaders inspire us to find that Picasso. They raise the ceiling on what we think is possible. They inspire us to believe that if we can dream it, we can do it.

Don't Confuse Performance with Potential

Alfred Oberlander had an idea that he believed would transform the performance of sales teams.[1] As manager of the Metropolitan Life Insurance Company offices in Rockaway, N.J., in 1961, Oberlander believed that a high-performing team of great sales agents, unencumbered by less talented performers, would improve sales dramatically. He had observed how much faster outstanding insurance agencies grew than average agencies. As his business expanded, he decided to reorganize the agents in his district based on their performance.[2]

He started by grouping all of the high performers into a single office with a high-performing manager. He then challenged these high-potential, top performers to produce at an unprecedented rate. The average performers were assigned to work for an average manager, while the lowest performers were given the least capable manager. Oberlander hoped that the average and low performers would continue to produce as they had in the past. He was confident that the high performers were going to flourish, driving overall sales to new heights.

Not surprisingly, he was right about the high performers. From the beginning, they performed at levels that even he had not anticipated. As their confidence grew, they began to call themselves the "super staff" in recognition of their performance. The super staff's performance was the primary reason why the region's sales grew by 40% in the first year.

Oberlander's 'dream team' hypothesis proved to be correct—to a point. The best, working with the best, set sales records. His hope that the lowest performers would maintain existing sales levels turned out to be wishful thinking. Saddled with less effective management and surrounded by others who saw themselves as underperformers, they underperformed. It did not take long for them to get the message that little was expected of them, and they took the message to heart. The low performers took fewer risks. They didn't work to close sales, and attrition within the group increased as their underperformance became habitual.

The average group, however, didn't get the memo that they were average. The manager deemed average by Oberlander refused to believe that she and the group she led were average. She would not accept that they were less capable or less talented than the super staff. She told her group that they had more potential than the top-performing group, but just lacked the years of experience selling insurance. Her beliefs about the potential of the team were continually communicated in her words and actions. Successes were celebrated. She treated the members of the team like high performers. And, much to Oberlander's surprise, they refused to be average. They became substantially higher performers. As the group gained in confidence, the rate at which they improved exceeded that of the super staff.

Oberlander's belief that the best performers would perform best in an environment where they were not saddled with the dilatory effects of mediocrity proved to have merit. High-performing teams simply don't accept average performance as "good enough." But it was Oberlander's underappreciation of the effect of leader expectations on performance that made his story memorable and led to decades of studies investigating the relationship between leader expectations and performance. Oberlander's experience led people to ask:

- How much better might people perform if leaders were to believe that ordinary people are capable of greatness?
- How much of the waste of human potential that occurs on our teams is the result of leader expectations that underestimate that potential?

Why Do We Expect So Little from So Many?

Are average performers average because they are less talented? Or, do they appear less talented because they are considered average and treated as average?

This was among the questions that led Harvard Professor Robert Rosenthal and Lenore Jacobson, an elementary school principal just south of San Francisco, to study the effects of teacher expectations on student performance. They sought to assess how much student performance could be accelerated if teachers thought students were smart and ready to learn and how much a teacher's low expectations inhibit student learning.[3]

The first step in their research design was to test all of the students at the beginning of the year using an IQ test that they called the Test of General Ability, or TOGA. The teachers were told that the test was the Harvard Test of Inflected Acquisition. The teachers were told, falsely, that the test could predict which students were likely to "bloom" in the coming year. Academic "blooming," the teachers were told, measured a student's readiness to enter a "period of increased learning abilities" within the next year. The reality, not shared with the teachers, was that the Test of Inflected Acquisition had no ability to predict future student performance.

Eighteen teachers were told that they were being entrusted with students who scored in the top 20 percent on the test and that these students were ready to "bloom." In reality, the teachers were given a random sampling of students so that the only differences in student ability would be in the minds of the teachers.

As the researchers expected, the teachers treated students who they believed scored in the top 20 percent on the test differently from the others. Teachers paid more attention to them. They called on them more frequently. They built closer relationships with them, provided more feedback, and held the students more accountable.

At the end of the school year, the students were re-tested, and the results confirmed Rosenthal's hypothesis that teacher expectations had a significant effect on student performance. The students who the teachers thought were most ready to learn learned significantly faster. Teacher expectations had become a self-fulfilling prophecy in the same way that Oberlander's "average" manager's high expectations had become self-fulfilling in the insurance industry. Rosenthal's work spurred more studies that attempted to test the effects of expectations on performance. Not surprisingly, the vast majority of these studies demonstrated that a leader's high expectations can significantly boost performance.

If we accept the hypothesis that high expectations can lead to higher performance, we are left to wonder why high expectations are so rare. Why did the teachers in the Oak School expect so little from students until researchers identified the "ready to bloom" students? Why do teachers limit the number of As that they give in their classes when they know that might communicate to the other students that only a small portion of the class is smart enough to earn an A? Why do leaders commonly expect that lower-level service workers won't willingly take responsibility? Why do so many companies require employees to get approvals for simple common-sense decisions? Why is it common for leaders to overreact to one person's transgressions and create rules that communicate distrust in the hope that no other person will ever make that mistake again?

We don't believe there is an easy, universal answer to the question of why we expect so little from so many talented people. It is clear that some leaders' low expectations of some people are deeply held. The refrains are not uncommon:

> *"You don't understand the students today. They have no work ethic. They don't care about learning."*
>
> *"The people who apply for these jobs are just looking for a paycheck. You can't expect them to be highly motivated."*
>
> *"You need to have incentives for these people. Why else would they work?"*

But not all communications of low expectations are purposeful. Some are the result of people who are on management autopilot. They perpetuate practices that send the message that "we don't expect too much" without being aware of the message they are sending or the effect that the message might have on performance.

As leaders, we need to be more mindful of the many ways we communicate our expectations and we must be more aware of the power inherent in our beliefs about people. The price that we are paying for moderating our expectations is far too high. Certainly, there is risk in expecting so much that we appear unreasonable. However, every act of innovation probably looks unreasonable until someone proves it to be possible. To paraphrase an old saw: the biggest danger is not that our expectations are too high and we fail to meet them; the biggest risk is that our expectations are too low and we do meet them.

What Smart Rats Can Teach Us About High Expectations

When we authentically believe in the potential of people and we genuinely desire to communicate that we believe they are capable of greatness, letting people know that we believe in them comes naturally. We trust them. We delegate responsibility. We greet them warmly. We ensure that they have the tools and support they need to be successful. We provide feedback while ensuring they know that we have their best interests at heart. When we are effective, the reaction that we get can be magical.

What is less apparent to most of us, however, is that even when we are not trying to communicate our expectations, we're doing so in ways that may not be obvious. Our words, actions, and expressions send messages that most people have the innate ability to decipher effectively. People can read our minds and our body language, often before we say a word. Our expectations are always communicated, albeit often unknowingly and unintentionally.

Two studies published in 1967 by UCLA professor Albert Mehrabian concluded that more than 90 percent of the messages we communicate have remarkably little to do with what we say. He concluded that of the messages we convey, 55 percent are communicated through body language (facial expressions, gestures, postures, etc.), 38 percent through tone of voice, and only 7 percent through words.[4] Similarly, Oxford professor Michael Argyle found that nonverbal forms of communication are 12.5 times more powerful in communicating interpersonal attitudes and feelings than are verbal forms.[5]

The inescapable fact is that most of us have great BS detectors. We can smell inauthenticity a mile away. We know this because we have all had the opportunity, or misfortune, to meet a person who tells us something but doesn't really believe it. It may have been a used-car salesperson who told us that a car had never had a problem. Or, it may have been the coach who tried to convince us that he or she had confidence in our ability to perform, or, the teacher who told us that we were smart. Despite their best efforts at persuasion, we could read in their eyes that they didn't believe what they were telling us. The truth is that when it comes to our beliefs, if we try to fake it or don't authentically believe what we're saying, we come off as disingenuous. Often, we just end up looking like fools.

Masking our true feelings is impossible. In his Pygmalion article published in the Harvard Business Review, J. Sterling Livingston offers a powerful reminder that even in our silence, we send very clear and unambiguous messages:

> *A manager often communicates most when he believes he is communicating least. For instance, when he says nothing, when he becomes 'cold' and 'uncommunicative', it usually is a sign that he (or she) is displeased. The silent treatment communicates negative feelings even more effectively, at times, than a tongue lashing does. What seems to be critical in the communication of expectations is not what the boss says, so much as the way he behaves.*[6]

If you hold even a glimmer of belief that you are the rare leader who can effectively convince people that you believe in their ability to do great things when you don't, a study performed by Professor Rosenthal that preceded his work at the Oak School should provide a sobering taste of reality. In this study, Rosenthal attempted to gauge the impact of researcher expectations or researcher bias by introducing "smart rats" into a maze-running experiment.[7]

In this experiment, research assistants were divided into two groups. One group was told that they had been given all of the smart rats—"maze bright" rats as they were called. The other group was told that they had been given the supposedly less intelligent "maze dull" rats. Yes, this really happened, and yes, it seems that the researchers believed the professor when he described the relative intelligence of the rats.

In actuality, Rosenthal had randomly distributed to the groups the only kind of rats he had: standard-issue lab rats. Sure enough, the group of Harvard students who believed they had the smart rats consistently outperformed the group that believed they had rats of inferior intelligence. Somehow, some way, the rats got the message. The expectations of the researchers affected the performance of the rats. Presumably, the rats understood many of the nonverbal clues that comprise 90 percent of what we understand from any communication.

The primary message we take from Rosenthal's "Smart Rat Experiment" is quite simple. If standard-issue lab rats can interpret the beliefs of researchers, then it should be obvious that the people on our teams will understand our beliefs whether we want them to or not. People are always communicating. We know when people believe in us and when they don't. It's important to understand that if we, as leaders, are crazy enough to try to convince people of anything inauthentically, the one thing that we are likely to convince them of is that we are not very effective leaders.

15 for 15—Confidence Matters

When we communicate our expectations, confidence matters. To be effective, leaders must not only believe in the capability of their teams to perform, but also have confidence in their ability to lead and to influence others to follow. They must believe that they are capable of leading people to do extraordinary things.

Confidence is one of those words that can mean different things to different people. The type of confidence we're talking about is *not* the kind rooted in bravado or an inappropriately large ego. The kind of confidence that we are advocating is the sort that is manifested in the performance of a team rather than in the personality of its leader. It is persuasive because it is authentic. It is more passionate than boastful. It is heartfelt and contagious.

This is the type of confidence that is required to consistently challenge people to raise their games in pursuit of a worthy cause. Unfortunately, there are precious few leaders who exude the kind of self-confidence that is required to inspire a team to consistently achieve remarkable results. It is far more common to hear leaders say that they are confident and optimistic but then watch as they spend hours explaining why change is difficult and takes far more time than people realize.

It is possible that less confident leaders are simply more realistic. There is plenty of research that demonstrates that optimistic leaders tend not to be realists. And there are many reasons to hedge our bets. It is difficult to consistently challenge yesterday's notions of what's possible, to challenge existing cultural norms, and to create an environment where people are willing to learn their way into the future. Considering the track records of most leaders who have attempted to lead substantial change efforts, it's easy to make a strong argument that it would be crazy to be confident in one's ability to lead a team to transform its fortunes.

But, when you meet the rare leaders who possess that "crazy" kind of confidence in their team's ability to achieve greatness, their confidence is unmistakable. We learned that lesson in early 2015 when our friend Dabo Swinney tried to convince us that Clemson's football team was going to play for a national championship that very year.

"It's going to be 15 for 15," he told us. He said he told the team that "they were going to make the university print tickets for 15 games that year." He reminded us that the only way a college football team can play 15 games in a year is to make it to the National Championship Game, and, according to Dabo, that is precisely what Clemson was going to do.

We looked at each other. It had to be hyperbole. He had to be kidding. Clemson University had not been in a national championship game since 1981. The team did not have a returning starting lineman on offense or defense. The freshman quarterback, although immensely talented, was coming off a serious injury. Dabo could read the skepticism on our faces.

"Oh, you of little faith" he told us. He looked at us like we were crazy for even entertaining a doubt. He then went on to tell us why he was right and why we didn't get it. He was adamant: Clemson was going to the championship game. His confidence was unequivocal. Dabo was so convinced that when we left his house that night, he almost had us rethinking our thinking. We wanted to believe him, but in all honesty, we were doubtful. Clemson, one of the two best teams in the country in 2015? Wishful thinking, we thought.

At the end of that season, we found ourselves right where Dabo told us we would be: watching Clemson play for the national championship. What seemed like a dream seven months earlier was playing out in front of our eyes. Unfortunately for Clemson fans, the University of Alabama won the national championship that year in a close game. But it was, as Dabo had predicted, 15 in 15. It was far less surprising the following year when the Clemson football team again played 15 games and again made it to the national championship game. This time they beat Alabama. In 2017, the Tigers came one game short of going to the championship game three years in a row. Remarkably, it was 15 for 15 in 2018, as Clemson again won the National Championship by beating Alabama again.

We are not saying that every confident leader is as successful as the Clemson coach has been. However, what we are saying is that part of how high expectations and strong beliefs are effectively communicated is through the confidence of the leader. Confidence is contagious. Over time, confidence expands what members of a team think is possible. As confidence grows, what once seemed unattainable now seems likely. As team members experience more success, their mindsets begin to expand. Challenges don't seem quite as daunting. People start to believe more in their abilities and in the abilities of their teammates. What seemed crazy yesterday now seems not so far-fetched. A virtuous cycle is created in which each ensuing success builds on the last one and makes the next one more possible.

You doubt Dabo and other leaders who believe that the extraordinary is within their reach at your own peril. They won't be right all the time. Most fail many times before they succeed. But it is their confidence, combined with an unwavering belief in the goodness and ability of people, that is their competitive advantage. We admire them not just because they win games; we admire them because in the process of winning, they change lives.

Our Words are a Window to Our Beliefs

Given the research on the benefits of positive emotion and positive expectations, it's surprising how many cultures are rife with language almost certain to undermine team confidence.

We are not sure why we would value people who tend to be critical more than those who tend to be positive, but often we do. Research has demonstrated that most leaders are far better at communicating low expectations than high expectations. It shows that being critical, even when we're wrong, can make us seem smarter or more competent. It seems nonsensical that we would value people who communicate that people on their teams are not that talented and then work, unintentionally, to show us that they were right. But we do.

It's not that people intend to communicate critical messages just to be critical. In most cases, critical messages are communicated with the best of intentions, to help people correct problems and improve. However, when the preponderance of our communication is critical, the message sent can be one of systemically low expectations that make goal attainment more difficult. We need to become more mindful that the language we choose can be self-defeating. Often, what people hear is not what we intended to communicate. At other times, what people hear is exactly how we feel and what we would never want them to know:

- "That will be overwhelming to them."
  (They are not smart enough or mature enough or experienced enough or 'something' enough to deal with reality.)
- "You expect too much."
  (You can't expect excellence or expect people to change.)

- "They will never change."
  (This group is not capable enough or committed enough to change.)
- "Students don't care anymore."
  (If they were committed or if they cared like we do, they would not act the way they act. It's not our fault.)
- "You can't expect high school players to practice that much, or care that much..."
  (They are only in high school. To expect them to learn and practice or to care about excellence is a bridge too far.)

Maybe the words that have the most power and longest-lasting effect are labels that are applied as personal descriptors. Labels matter—especially to the person being labeled. It should not be surprising how often someone labeled a "non-singer," or a "non-athlete," or a "non-A student," becomes what they have been labeled. Okay, maybe it's true that a person can't sing well today. Still, being told you are a non-singer at 12 doesn't help your prospects. It should not surprise us that Little League players who get labeled as "poor players" compared with their peers often end up quitting the game before they have a chance to develop. Nor should it surprise us that grading others as "average performers" in performance appraisals often leads to higher turnover and more average performance.

Our words matter. Because they are a window to our souls, the power and influence of our words can be long-lasting. Even casual comments are impactful. Choose carefully. People understand that words are not just words; they are a glimpse into our beliefs. The more significant our position on the team, the more we are liked, and the more competent we are, the greater the effect our words are likely to have.

Smart Goals May Not be that Smart

Traditional management wisdom tells us that a leader's expectations must pass the "reality test" before high expectations can translate into higher levels of performance. The idea is that people simply will not commit to aspirations that are unattainable. This notion is consistent with the theory of achievement motivation advanced by researchers David McClelland of Harvard and John Atkinson of Michigan.[8] They found that "no motivation or response is aroused when the goal is perceived as being either virtually certain or virtually impossible to attain."

This research led people to build goal-setting models designed to help people communicate high, but attainable, expectations of performance. Most commonly, these models are variations of a process known as setting SMART goals. This model advocates setting goals that are Specific, Measurable, Attainable, Relevant, and Trackable. The SMART acronym has been repeated so many times that it is almost a reflexive response for many leaders. For them, it seems like common sense to ensure that expectations are attainable. But is it common sense in a world where innovation is changing what we think is attainable at a record pace?

It is hard to disagree that goals should be specific, relevant, measurable and trackable. Specificity and relevancy improve and enable commitment as well as collective action. Measurable and trackable goals are required to provide specific feedback that can facilitate learning. But how about attainable? Does attainable mean that our goals must be achievable within the present process? Using current methods? Can something reasonably be perceived as attainable if it has not been done before? Don't most innovative solutions seem unreasonable and unattainable when viewed through a pragmatic lens anchored in present practices?

We can't help but wonder if setting SMART goals can be limiting in cultures where goals are seen as commitments and predictability is valued over experimentation. And that, of course, is most cultures. If we intend to create cultures that support innovation, then we have to set goals that stretch our imaginations, invite conflict, and require experimentation. Attainability, if we choose to continue to use that term, must be redefined in a way that embraces uncertainty and makes us uncomfortable. Of course, that may strike us as a counterproductive way to set goals in settings where we are dependent on achieving a known goal to maximize compensation. But, the solution is not to set more moderate goals and expect innovation. It is to set more aggressive goals, understanding that the goals are innovation and learning rather than complete certainty.

SMART may be a simple construct in that it is easy to understand, easy to teach, and a catchy acronym to use when talking about goal-setting. However, in a world that requires innovation for survival, SMART goals may not be all that smart. Thinking that goals must be attainable within the present process leads many to regularly negotiate for goals that allow people to "hold on" to past practices. This is especially true when these goals are the foundation of pay-for-performance processes that encourage negotiating for goals that are conservative and require little change. The predictable result of moderate expectations is chronic underperformance. In light of the failures of past practice, we could do with a little unreasonableness in our goal-setting, for as George Bernard Shaw reminded us, "All progress depends on the unreasonable man."

The Young and Inexperienced are the Most Affected

The first days on a job can affect people's work lives for years. Some companies know it and take steps to effectively integrate new employees into the organization. Some companies know it and find a reason not to act. Most don't realize that their expectations of performance have the greatest impact on the newly hired, especially if they are young and inexperienced.

The new and inexperienced are more impressionable and more affected by the expectations of others, because they have yet to form a strong opinion as to what they believe they can achieve in their new situation. The older and more experienced, on the other hand, have usually developed a far more rigid belief system. Their experience often leads them to think that they know their abilities and limitations. The battle scars of their past skirmishes serve as a reminder of the dangers inherent in challenging cultural norms. They are often perceived to be set in their ways for good reason.

The best teams and the best organizations understand that the first days on the team present a never-to-be-repeated opportunity to socialize new members in a safe, supportive environment that communicates high expectations. They take onboarding and the mentoring of new employees seriously, leaving very little to chance. We can still remember our first "Traditions One" class at Disney. We found ourselves fully immersed in the onboarding program taught by a cast member who lived Disney's values in a way that had us feeling like we were part of the cast. Nothing was left to chance. History. Traditions. Culture. Going through the program and listening to them talk about the mission of the company was pride-evoking. When we left that day, we felt as though we had to live up to the examples of the cast members who had come before us. The bar was raised. We felt responsible.

Over the years, we could not help but notice that many of the leaders who we worked with in Silicon Valley got their start at Hewlett Packard. Many were engineers who had come to the Valley to participate in a tech revolution and found themselves learning the ropes through an onboarding process known as the "HP Way."[9] HP indoctrinated new workers in the values, behaviors, and principles that made the company special. HP would not let people come to work on the first day without pre-assigned work and a real deadline. The initial assignment with accountability on day one sent a strong message: we knew you were coming, you are important, and you are accountable. High expectations were clearly and unmistakably communicated from the start. That message was further buttressed by exemplars in how to live the HP way who were hand-picked to mentor new hires. Again, very much like Disney, nothing was left to chance. In retrospect, no one should be surprised, that in the early days, a large percentage of executives in Silicon Valley started at HP.

Most companies talk about onboarding programs but don't take them seriously. Too often, new hires are put through an HR class that is more administrative than values-driven. They are assigned to leaders who are often not exemplars, and they are introduced to processes that evoke more mediocrity than excellence. It should surprise no one that most people are less motivated after three months on the job than they were the first day at work. It need not be that way. We are most impressionable when we first show up, before we have been socialized by cultural experiences in the workplace.

Research on the effects of our 'first bosses' further highlights the benefits of paying attention to the power of initial impressions. The effects of our first days and weeks on the job last for years. Why would we ever allow people that we have spent time and money recruiting come to work only to find that their new supervisor doesn't lead in ways that are consistent with their aspirations? Why wouldn't we ensure that new members of the team learn from the best? Are we ever really too busy to ensure that new team members are given the best chance at succeeding? Whichever path we choose, the one thing that seems clear from the research is that the effects of these decisions will be felt for years.

When High Expectations Can be Hazardous to Your Career Health

When we think about the accomplishments of some of the great teams that we have studied and visited, it is clear that even the leaders of those teams would not have expected the level of success that their teams achieved. Over time, however, success can cause expectations to grow. Yesterday's successes make tomorrow's more likely. And every success leads us to expect more, to practice harder, and to demand more of ourselves as we learn to believe that remarkable is within our reach.

When a young teacher from Colombia was hired to teach math in an inner-city high school in East Los Angeles, few people expected his students to excel.[10] As Jaime Escalante took over as chair of the math program at Garfield High in 1974, AP Calculus was not offered, student performance in lower-level classes was suspect, the school's accreditation was threatened, and graduation was seen as a stretch goal. He was warned not to try to teach calculus, as most students had not shown the aptitude to pass algebra. Like most effective leaders, though, Escalante refused to be conditioned by what others believed was possible.

In 1978, the year in which AP Calculus was first taught at Garfield, it was cause for celebration when two of the five students in the class passed the AP test. What people did not understand was that the wheel of achievement was just beginning to turn. Escalante was beginning to transform a classroom of individuals into a confident team willing to defy the expectations of an entire community. Even the Educational Testing Service was taken aback. When 18 students passed the AP test in 1982, ETS challenged the results, but all who retook the test passed. The momentum continued to build. The next year, participation nearly doubled; 33 students took the exam and 30 passed. In 1987, 73 students passed the AP Calculus Test at Garfield and 12 passed the far more difficult BC version of the test. What was once perceived by most as the unrealistic expectation of a "new teacher" who did not understand the limitations of the culture was now a movement whose momentum seemed unstoppable—right up until it stopped.

The movie *Stand and Deliver* that purported to tell Escalante's story told neither the entire strength of Garfield's math achievements nor how one of the most remarkable educational achievements of our lifetime came unraveled in a storm of political controversy. By 1990, Escalante's math enrichment program had grown to more than 400 students and AP class sizes had swelled as more and more students learned they could compete academically. As the program grew, so did the resistance to the changes inherent in these successful transformations. Escalante got death threats and he lost chairmanship of the math department as internal political squabbles increased. The teachers union began to criticize what was happening when Escalante wanted to increase classes to sizes that would exceed the bargained-for maximum of 50 students. Eventually, the organizational white blood cells came and stamped out the infection. In 1991, Escalante left Garfield. Soon thereafter, other teachers in the math department followed suit. Within a few years, a school that had risen to the top ten in the nation in the number of students passing the AP exam saw the number passing the test decline by nearly 80 percent—proof that you can kill a great team in a fraction of the time it takes to build one.

The Escalante experience still guides much of our thinking, not just because he led a transformation in learning. His experience stands as a constant reminder of how a person with high expectations of performance can be seen as a deviant among a group of leaders who do not share the same expectations or beliefs. Cultures tend to be self-protective. Cultural pressures to get people to conform are real and persistent. They undermined even a successful teacher who had become a cultural icon.

Maybe the reason we have so many cultures that perpetuate moderate expectations is that so many cultures expect so little from so many. Creating a culture of systemically high expectations will not come easily for most. Far too often, we have been too tolerant of being slightly above average. Increasing our innovative abilities will require that we raise our expectations of what is possible significantly. It will require nearly every leader to change and it will require that we rethink management processes that were developed in an era where conformity was more valuable. It will often require that we summon the courage to withstand the pressures that are likely to come from those who don't want to change or who don't believe that, in a given situation, greatness is within reach. To achieve remarkable, we must expect remarkable.

Chapter 4 | Summary

1. High expectations are the secret of great teams. The best leaders refuse to accept explanations of our limitations. They often demand more from us than we think is possible, and they support our efforts to achieve. As we get with their programs, we begin to believe that more is possible. Unleashed from the shackles of our past limitations, we achieve more. These achievements then lead us to believe that even more is achievable tomorrow, and a virtuous cycle is accelerated that can lead a team to greatness.
2. We must become more aware of how we limit our expectations of people's capabilities unnecessarily. From grades in school, to who can take advanced placement tests, to how many top ratings can be awarded for work performance, many of our existing processes communicate to people that they should not aim too high. Such built-in barriers ignore a long history of people outperforming what others thought possible. We have seen the walk-on athlete catch the pass to win the national championship and the school dropout start a billion-dollar business. By now, it is common knowledge that the best basketball player on this planet and global icon was cut from his high school JV team.
3. The only way to communicate high expectations is to actually have high expectations. We communicate our beliefs about the ability of others even when we think we are not doing so. We can't hide our beliefs. People know what we think of them even before we complete

a sentence. Thinking we can BS people about our expectations is BS.

4. The most successful teams do not communicate their expectations solely by aiming at success. Success doesn't come to us because we seek it. It comes to us as a result of our passion for excelling at a cause we deem worthy. It is always a byproduct of our expectations, hard work, and a supportive process that encourages learning and development.
5. Challenging cultural expectations can be hazardous to your career health. Culture works to perpetuate yesterday's norms and beliefs. It is important to maintain relationships in the existing culture and to build an environment where people feel safe in challenging themselves to do more. There is a fine line between challenging people to give their best and what can be perceived as placing unrealistic demands. People want to excel but won't do so when fear limits the risks that they are willing to take.

Make Accountability Mutual

"He that is good for making excuses is seldom good for anything else."
– Benjamin Franklin

"A body of men holding themselves accountable to nobody ought not to be trusted by anybody."
– Thomas Paine

Performance matters. You can't win the game if people don't consistently play at a high level. This is true in the classroom. It is true in the boardroom. People need to be accountable for their performance, for giving their best. If a team has any hope of achieving significant results, accountability must be the cornerstone of high performance and confidence. About this, there is little disagreement or debate.

However, over the years, we have become acutely aware that accountability means very different things to different people. For many, accountability is a leadership responsibility, a means to ensure that every person performs at a high level. Too often, however, inherent in this kind of leader-focused accountability is an unarticulated undercurrent of fear and punishment. Most leaders don't like to believe they threaten or bribe people to act responsibly. But often, they do.

- "We need to hold them accountable. We are carrying far too many non-performers."
- "If they can't do the job, we will find someone who can."
- "Rank-order them. Reward the ones at the top. More accountability for those at the bottom."
- "Every year let's just fire the bottom ten percent. That will make everyone strive to get better. That's accountability."

We may not agree with these statements, but each of these has been expressed to us by senior managers in the last six months. Holding others accountable in one form or another has become so prevalent in our leadership lexicon that it is now considered a valued leadership competency. However, in our quest for greater accountability, we may have overlooked the unintended, fear-inducing effects of many of these processes. When we view accountability as primarily a management responsibility, something that we "*do to others*," we're traveling a path that is unlikely to result in greater engagement and innovation.

We believe that there is a different, more effective kind of accountability, the kind of accountability that we have witnessed on nearly every high-performing team we've met over the last decade. These teams don't view accountability as primarily a management responsibility. On these teams, everyone is accountable. It is more about maximizing potential than ensuring compliance. Fear-inducing processes and practices are not weaponized to try and make things predictable. The fear that exists on these teams is not a fear of being held to account but rather a fear of letting the team down. On these teams, accountability is a commitment that every team member makes to do their best and to ensure that everyone on the team does the same.

This is not to say that accountability is a soft, touchy-feely concept. On the best teams, accountability can be harsh, direct, and unwavering. These teams are less tolerant of intentional transgressions of team values. People are expected to step up to new challenges, to hold others accountable for bringing their "A" game every day. Moreover, individuals who demonstrate an unwillingness to make that level of commitment are often asked to leave before their attitudes can impact team culture. Yet, somehow on these teams, the "knee-knocking" accountability that characterizes their culture is more energizing than fear-inducing.

How is this possible? How can we lead with love and still have knee-knocking accountability without fearful undertones? The answer lies in the involvement of the entire team in making accountability mutual.

Mutual Accountability Means Everyone is Responsible

Last spring, we were watching a college football practice when a fight broke out. During a scrimmage, two players started pushing, shoving, and trash-talking. We were not surprised that emotions boiled over during the full-contact scrimmage. What was surprising, however, is what happened next. Before any coach could intervene, the other players not only broke up the confrontation, but several of the more senior players told the practice field combatants, in no uncertain terms, that their behavior was out of line. "This is not who we are. It may happen elsewhere, but it is not acceptable here." Then, with some colorful words that we probably shouldn't repeat, the players sent their emotional teammates off the field, all before the coaches could get involved.

Later in the practice, the combatant players re-entered the scrimmage. As they came out into the huddle, they were hugged by their teammates, as if to say, "We are over it. You have learned your lesson, now let's get back to work."

"Best is the Standard" is written on the banner that hangs atop this team's practice facility. These players, through their actions, made it clear that this team's best did not include intra-squad fights in scrimmages.

Players holding each other accountable is, unfortunately, still not the norm. It is far more common for players to look to coaches to hold team members accountable. Compare the reactions of these college football players with those of some college baseball players we witnessed on a road trip several years ago. The baseball team was playing a weekend series against a conference rival. The team's curfew was clear: be in the hotel by 11p.m. As we watched the players return to the hotel on Friday night, every member of the team was in their assigned room by 11. However, by 11:30, almost half the team had left the hotel and made their way back to town to explore the nightlife. For these players, the 11 p.m. curfew was not their standard, but a rule they had to obey, albeit temporarily.

Weeks later, we had a chance to discuss the curfew rules with several senior players. They reassured us that everyone had obeyed the curfew. They were in their rooms by 11. We then confided that we had watched them leave shortly after the coach had done room checks. They gave a sort of embarrassed chuckle. Knowing they had been caught red-handed, they explained, "The rule didn't say that we had to stay there all night. Coach never checks after 11."

These two examples highlight one of the major differences between the type of accountability practiced on most teams and a form of accountability that is practiced on the elite teams we've encountered. On the best teams, accountability is not a management activity; it is a shared responsibility.

At the football practice the players held each other accountable. Accountability was everyone's job. It was a promise each player made when he became part of that team. On the baseball team, accountability was the coach's responsibility. The curfew was not a commitment made by players. The players were doing only what was necessary to stay out of trouble. It was the expectations of the leader that set the standard. The coach sent the message of what was expected, as well as the consequences that might be expected if players got caught. The coach assumed the role of goal-setter and disciplinarian.

We should not be surprised that when coaches or managers or teachers make and enforce the rules, people feel less committed and less accountable.

Creative Tension Can Create a Sense of Urgency

It is the responsibility of the leader to ensure that every person on the team is accountable for creating both a shared understanding of what the team hopes to accomplish and a shared understanding of the realities of present performance. Only when a team can focus on the gap between where it is today and where it hopes to be tomorrow can it hope to build an urgent commitment to change and overcome the team's natural preference for seeking the certainty of past practices.

A number of processes can help the team develop a shared sense of reality. Culture, engagement, and climate surveys have become common methods for kick-starting conversations that can help unearth important issues. Off-sites that address issues that can be triaged can be useful. We prefer culture assessments that don't simply rely on quantitative surveys. Although useful in making comparisons among companies, quantitative surveys alone reveal little about *why* people feel as they do in a specific company.

Using a tool that uncovers hidden or hard-to-talk-about issues is important given the fact that the most powerful cultural pressures are usually tacit and unarticulated. It is critical to remember that whatever tool is chosen, it cannot fully illuminate present reality. Its purpose is to create a conversation among team members so that, together, they can unearth the good, the bad, and the ugly of present performance and practices. No data-gathering tool can fully describe why we feel as we do, and no team will accept survey results without dialogue and debate.

Our ability to create a shared sense of reality is dependent upon our commitment to dialogues that are honest and transparent. Increased collective self-awareness, even in a relatively safe environment, creates significant tension and challenges the stability of our relationships. The tension that is created is not a static tension; it is a process of constant inquiry. It takes time. It is not for the thin-skinned or for the faint of heart. For it to be effective, there will be conflict and disagreements, even arguments. As one of our clients has put it, "If the process is working, glass will be broken. People's feelings will be hurt. People will be uncomfortable. The tension will be palpable. It is our passion for what we are trying to achieve that must give our conversations purpose."

Only when every member of the team becomes accountable for helping to maintain a level of creative tension based on a mutual understanding that today's practices are insufficient to support future success will they be likely to feel more in control and less controlled by the process. Creative tension kick-starts a dialogue that increases our ability to become learners in furtherance of our collective cause.

Holding our vision for the future and a shared understanding of present reality at the same time is fundamental to creating an urgency to change. We need to become more comfortable in the discomfort that comes with the realization that we will not find tomorrow's answers on yesterday's maps.

We must be mutually accountable for developing a shared understanding of:

- What we intend to accomplish in the future,
- Why these changes are important, and

- The realities of present performance and culture.

Creating a Shared Sense of Reality is Hard Work

Max De Pree, retired CEO at Herman Miller, liked to say that *the first responsibility of the leader is to see reality*, because he realized that without a shared, fact-based understanding of today's performance, substantial future improvement in team performance was unlikely.[1] It is simple advice, rarely heeded. For many, the temptation to see present performance through rose-colored glasses is irresistible. We like to think that we are doing a good job, that we are improving, and that we are making a difference. From the time we were children, we developed—at times almost perfected—a set of defensive routines designed to insulate us from a full understanding of how we helped create the present challenges we face. Because we don't want to feel that we are underperforming or squandering our resources, we tend to pull friendly information close and explain away discomforting information.

After years of practice, our defensive routines are well developed. Most of us have become so adept at calling on these routines that we no longer even realize that we are being defensive.

- "I'm not being defensive, these are just the facts."
- "We tried to fix the problem, but they just wouldn't listen."

- "If they would just (fill in the blank), then we would . . ."
- "I'm not sure he knows what is really going on."

The list of responsibility-deflecting responses is limited only by our imaginations. At times we seem to have forgotten De Pree's reminder that "the truth is the truth even when spoken by the biggest ass in the room."

Recently, the CEO of a market-leading, mid-size business was walking the halls of the company discussing the results of a cultural audit designed to offer an unbiased view of present performance. He was struck by the number of people who were interested in questioning the efficacy of the report. It seemed that more people wanted to deny the report's findings than to learn from what it exposed about their cultural weaknesses.

- "You can't believe this stuff."
- "Look at how few people they interviewed."
- "We are not that bad."
- "They don't understand our business."
- "We are much better than we used to be."

The CEO found few partners in his quest to highlight the realities of present performance. He found, albeit in a time-consuming way, that increasing a group's self-awareness can be more difficult in practice than in theory. As difficult as it can be for individuals to seek discomforting information, the challenge of increasing the self-awareness of a group is made even more difficult because nearly every group's culture has built-in protection mechanisms that kick in to protect the group from disruptive influences. And that is true even if the disruption is just an honest assessment of the group's vulnerabilities.

The reality is that most smart and competent people are better at recognizing and solving *other people's problems.* Most are far less willing to recognize their complicity in the creation of those problems. The result of their unwillingness to consider a different, less comfortable point of view can result in more blame, less recognition of reality, and widespread advocacy for the safe harbor of yesterday's performance.

Mutual Accountability as the Foundation of Outrageous Performance

When a team becomes mutually accountable for committing to a cause, looking reality in the eye, and giving its best effort every day, the results can far exceed even the team's or the coach's wildest expectations. When we become accountable for seeking evidence-based feedback, learning is accelerated and individual and team performance improves. Today's successes beget more success tomorrow. Momentum continues to grow, and the team's celebrations become more frequent, even as its members become more honest and more direct in their assessment of present shortcomings. As a result, they become tougher competitors. They seem to start every game with a couple of runs on the scoreboard.

By all accounts, few cultures are as mutually accountable and as brutally honest in their assessments of performance as the one led by Anson Dorrance, the University of North Carolina's women's soccer coach. When he took over as women's coach in 1979 (he was already the men's coach), he committed to building a different kind of competitive culture, one not often seen in women's sports at the time.[2]

Candid. Tough. Competitive. The UNC women's soccer program developed a culture in which every practice move was recorded and graded. Feedback was respectful but brutally honest. UNC's culture and the success that followed changed the landscape of women's soccer at all levels. It attracted the most talented athletes and made the best players even better. The creative tension inherent in this culture was undoubtedly uncomfortable for some. This culture, like most other high performing cultures, is not for everyone. But, for the ones who embraced UNC's highly competitive culture, Chapel Hill became a place of realized potential.

Not even Anson Dorrance could have anticipated the success that this culture engendered. Over the next four decades, the UNC women's team would win over 90 percent of its games, losing on average just over one game a year and winning 21 national championships. Over the 36-year history of the women's soccer program, the Tar Heels have won nearly 90%

of their games, 22 of 27 ACC titles and 22 of 36 NCAA championships. The success of this program has been sustained over more than nine generations of players and during a time when the women's game has changed significantly.

Yes, UNC has recruited great players. You can't win without talent. But when you talk to opposing coaches, they are quick to point out that what has made UNC so tough goes far beyond talent. They believe that the program's success is cultural. They say it was apparent from the inception of the program that Dorrance's teams approached the game differently. They believe that the Tar Heels helped redefine the women's game by bringing a level of aggression to the soccer pitch that had never been seen before.

What is less obvious about the Tar Heel culture is that, despite the highly competitive environment, Dorrance and his players had developed, in their words, a family atmosphere. They were guided by their commitment to "accountability, collaboration, and initiative." Their values statement provides insight into how great teams invite people to make a maximum contribution in an environment where accountability is mutual and the creative tension is both uncomfortable and energizing.

> *We don't whine. We work hard. The truly extraordinary do something every day. We choose to be positive. When we don't play as much as we would like, we are noble and still support the team and its mission. We don't freak out over*

ridiculous issues or live in fragile states of emotional catharsis or create crises where none should exist. We are well led. We care about each other as teammates and human beings. We play for each other. And we want our lives (and not just in soccer) to be never-ending ascensions.[3]

Core Values and Mutual Accountability

A few years ago, we were in a meeting with the top management team of a large American company that had just undergone a transition in ownership from the founder to a large strategic buyer. The meeting was convened to discuss the results of a recent cultural audit we had conducted. The management team wanted to ensure that throughout the transition it would not lose its shared values. The team believed that these values were the glue that held it together and allowed management to retain top talent.

As the management team sat to discuss the audit findings, the CEO asked the group to name the core values of the company, the ones hanging on walls throughout their offices, the values that were supposed to guide their decision-making. After struggling for a few minutes to list those values, the group finally recreated the list. The CEO then asked the group to rate, on a scale from 1 to 10 (low to high), the extent to which they were living these values. (The values had been central to the message of the company's founder for nearly 20 years.)

The room went silent; nobody seemed to want to make eye contact. The tension was palpable. Finally, one member of the team shared that she would rate her commitment to living the company's values at about a 5 on a 10 point scale. She continued, "I believe we say that these values are important. But come on, we don't live them. Hell, we really can't even remember them."

That led another manager to respond. His message was a similar one. For the next several minutes, going around the long table, each person in attendance rated their adherence to the company's values. The average score of the management team was a smidge less than 5. Their explanations were instructive:

- "We really don't think about these values much anymore. We are so busy. I think we take them for granted."
- "I don't think most people in the company can even list the values. I know they're posted somewhere, but I am not sure that new employees are ever told that they are important. I am sure that it doesn't enter their minds when they make decisions."
- "If we are going to be totally honest," one senior manager added, "I would say that we have compromised our commitment to quality. Truthfully, I feel like we are more committed to productivity than quality. Let's be honest, that's been our focus. Maybe part of our resistance to talking about these values is that we know that we don't live them."

- "Nobody holds us accountable for these values anymore. I am accountable for sales and expenses, not for values. So I guess, without someone holding us accountable, we have lost focus," one manager responded in a far-too-obvious attempt to deflect accountability.

Finally, one member of the team, obviously frustrated, changed the tenor of the conversation. "Let's get real. These are not someone else's values. These are our values. We are the leadership team. We're supposed to lead by example, and we are supposed to help others understand how important these values are to the company. I have failed our team. I've failed, not only because I failed to live the values. I've failed because I didn't confront you when I saw you not living them."

The room grew quiet. Everyone slowly nodded their heads in agreement. Coming to any other conclusion would have been difficult. Everyone in the room agreed that accountability for living their values was everyone's responsibility, and that all of them had failed to be responsible. Seemingly determined, every manager agreed to do better in the future. They agreed to hold each other accountable and they promised that they would consider the values of the company when making decisions.

The management team's new-found commitment lasted about a week. In a matter of days, their quality values again fell victim to the overarching push for efficiency. Only now, when we followed up with the managers about their commitment to representing the company's values, most of them did not want to discuss the issue. They were embarrassed. When they were willing to discuss the issues, some pointed at the CEO. "If he doesn't care enough to act, why should I?" Others took a different tack: "Why should I be the only one to call BS?" In this team's case, the values they espoused and the values they lived were different and weren't about to change.

Accountability cannot be someone else's job. It must be mutual. It must be everyone's responsibility. It must be a personal commitment. Accountability cannot be delegated to our teachers or our coaches or our managers. When we try to delegate that responsibility, we are starting down a road where accountability is an illusion. At its core, accountability is a set of mutual promises that reinforce the team's identity and make performance more predictable. When we overlook purposeful transgressions of our values even just once, our identity is weakened. Excusing transgressions of our core promises makes the next transgression more likely.

Structures that Support Accountability Can be One of a Kind

Bob Ladouceur, or Coach Lad as he is called, the head football coach at De La Salle High School in Concord, California, showed us how a team's commitment to mutual accountability could help change the dynamics of a team and the fortunes of a program. His remarkable leadership story has more to do with teaching young men how to be responsible teammates and citizens than it does about winning football games. That being said, De La Salle has won more than its share of games.

Many of the team's accomplishments were chronicled in the 2014 movie *When The Game Stands Tall.* The movie depicted some of the team dynamics during De La Salle's 12 consecutive undefeated seasons. It is a remarkable story of how a football team from a private, Catholic, all-boys high school won 151 games in a row while teaching athletes to be accountable. During Coach Lad's tenure as head coach, De La Salle's record was 399 wins, 25 losses, and 3 ties.

When we first interviewed Coach Lad, he was hesitant to talk about the 151-game winning streak, wanting to spend more time talking about the love he had for his players, (yes, he too used the word love) and how he tried to prepare each of them to become leaders in the future. He was humble and thoughtful. He went out of his way to downplay his role. He was adamant that the team's success had less to do with him and more to do with the culture of the football program. We were caught off guard when he told us that he had never given a pregame speech. "I don't really think they work," he told us. "And even if I was good at it (he didn't think he was) and I could muster up one good speech, then what would I do the next week?" He believed that the secret to the program's success was rooted in each team's commitment, preparation, and willingness to be accountable to each other.

As is the case with most great coaches, Coach Lad is big on accountability. He told us, "Every player has a duty to be accountable and to hold others to account." He described how the second- and third-string players are responsible for holding the starters accountable for technique and effort. Likewise, the starters are accountable and responsible for teaching and developing their replacements. Coach Lad knew that it would be impossible to win every game for 12 years if the next generation of athletes had not been developed before they had to be "game-ready."

At first we were skeptical when the coach described what he called the "accountability card process." On the evening before game day, players and coaches meet as a team. Every player is responsible for reading his goals for the week from an index card. As new players enter the program, coaches teach them how to set measurable, observable goals, which describe their personal goals for the upcoming game and for their development for the next week. After reading his goals, each player is required to hand the card to one of his teammates (not a coach) and to ask the teammate to hold him accountable. The following week, players are required to hold each other accountable for doing what they declared they would do. Each week, after assessing progress from the preceding week, the players would set new goals and ask to be held accountable again.

If this sounds like a story we may have embellished to make a point, we assure you we have not. Our first reaction after hearing the story was, *wow, did these high school players honestly take this seriously? How long was it before the novelty wore off?* However, to the De La Salle team, the accountability card process was not a novelty; it was central to who they were and how they prepared to play. Mutual accountability was at the core of their culture. They took the task seriously because it had become part of their identity. It became how they passed on their values to future generations of players, reinforced their work ethic, and gave greater meaning to what it meant to be part of the team.

We wondered what happened when players failed to meet their goals or when they failed to act responsibly. We wanted to know what would happen if the players failed to be accountable. We wanted to understand the real consequences faced by 15-18 year old boys who were to be accountable for their improvement goals week after week. Coach Lad's response mirrored the learning mentality of other great leaders we have interviewed: It's "not a big deal if they don't reach their goals in any given week. We just strive to do better the next week." He believes that these goals are not something that should create a risk of punishment, shame, or embarrassment. The goals are just a public declaration of the player's intention, made in a safe environment where their teammates will be there to help and support them.

"It's just what we do here," Coach Lad told us matter-of-factly. We again learned a lesson that has been repeated time and again as we interviewed great teams. *What appears a little too crazy or touchy-feely for some can be the foundation of success on other teams. Great teams are great because they don't act like everyone else.*

Embracing Type II Accountability

For much of his professional life, Winston Lord had been a United States diplomat and foreign policy expert. He helped shape U.S. diplomacy for the better part of 30 years. He served as United States Ambassador to China and as a special assistant to Secretary of State Henry Kissinger.

Recounting what it was like to work for Secretary Kissinger, Lord described a time when he had spent days preparing a foreign policy speech and delivered it directly to the secretary. The subsequent events tell a story of accountability and are best shared in Lord's own words:

> *He called me in the next day and said, "Is this the best you can do?" I said, "Henry, I thought so, but I'll try again." So, I go back. In a few days, another draft. He called me in the next day and he said, "Are you sure this is the best you can do?" I said, "Well, I really thought so. I'll try one more*

time." Anyway, this went on eight times, eight drafts. Each time he said, "Is this the best you can do?" So, I went in there with a ninth draft, and when he called me in the next day and asked me that same question, I really got exasperated, and I said, "Henry, I've beaten my brains out—this is the ninth draft. I know it's the best I can do. I can't possibly improve one more word." He then looked at me and said, "In that case, now I'll read it."[4]

A colleague shared this story with us to support his conviction that every person should be accountable for producing his or her best work. He wasted no time in expressing his frustration with how often leaders are willing to accept mediocrity and then act surprised at their teams' lackluster performances. His point: if you want people to do their best, then their best should be the standard to which they should hold themselves and others accountable.

Unfortunately, our best is rarely the standard. Several years ago, we were asked to do a cultural assessment for a large apparel company. As we sat with the senior leader in the organization, we outlined some of the findings that were inhibiting the company's ability to improve. Shortly after the beginning of the presentation, the leader interrupted to assure us that the organization had made progress over the preceding 12 months. "We have some challenges, but you have to understand, we are better than we were last year."

We were sure that he was probably right. Throughout our assessment process, we had heard the same line repeated by many people at all levels of the organization. As the people we interviewed related the frustration they felt, and the challenges they faced in trying to create change, most were compelled to remind us that "they were better than they used to be." At first, this seemed like a great reminder to celebrate the improvements they had made in the last year. However, after a while, it became obvious that the memorializing of past improvements was being used by some to explain the reasons for present underperformance and to moderate future expectations. In this case, the apparel company's mantra of "we are better than we used to be" was shorthand for "we are good enough"—good enough to get our bonus and good enough to meet our goals, even though good enough wasn't close to the group's potential.

In a simpler world, the incremental improvement signified by "good enough" might have been good enough. However, success in the future will likely demand more significant, faster, and more innovative changes. Success in the future will require every person to make a maximum contribution. A 20 percent improvement may not be good enough if a 50 percent improvement is possible. We can no longer afford to anchor our thinking and goals to past performance when we know that our past performance captured only a fraction of what was possible.

Years ago, Charles Handy, the British author and social philosopher, labeled the type of accountability best used to reach one's potential Type II accountability. Handy was drawing an analogy to Type I and Type II statistical errors. Type I errors are errors of commission: we did something wrong. Handy classified Type II errors as errors of omission. In these cases, we failed to perform as well as we could have.

Handy believed that this distinction was critical. He believed that Type I accountability could actually prevent the kind of experimentation that would be required to innovate. Type II accountability, on the other hand, might help us focus our efforts on what is possible though, as of yet, unachieved. Handy's warnings are more timely today than when he published them three decades ago. Designing accountability systems with the idea of not making mistakes is a mistake. At the same time, accepting performance simply because it is better than last year's can be shortsighted and life-threatening to organizations.

We must start asking, "Is this the best you can do?" If the answer is not "yes," we have not acted accountably. Our best, whatever that is, must be the standard. Those who thrive in the future will have succeeded because they refused to judge their performance by simply looking in the rearview mirror. For the best leaders, impossibility is a mission, never an excuse.

Leadership Accountability: 7 Questions Every Leader Must be Able to Answer

Our attempts to hold leaders accountable have not been very effective. Present practices in leadership accountability have been woefully unsuccessful in developing the type of leaders we need for the future and in holding bad leaders to account. For far too long we've allowed culture-killing leaders to persist in organizations, even though they regularly undermine team performance.

Eighty-six percent of respondents to a survey from the World Economic Forum believe that we're suffering a global leadership crisis.[5] It's time to rethink leadership accountability practices. We're not talking about a slight tweak around the edges or subtle, incremental changes. We must re-examine the basic, foundational principles upon which these practices were built.

The failings of many of our present practices are well-known. Nearly 70 years ago, MIT professor Douglas McGregor published the article *An Uneasy Look at Performance Appraisals*.[6] In that paper, he highlighted the discomfort that people felt with performance appraisal processes. McGregor noted that the appraisals, as designed, were not only uncomfortable for most to conduct but were largely ineffective. Seventy years later, little has changed. Most leadership appraisal and accountability assessments remain unpopular—and for good reason. Most are perceived to be time-consuming and ineffective, if not systemically unfair.

Over the years, we've nibbled around the edges, trying to improve these processes—little by little. We've changed what competencies should be evaluated, we've renamed the boxes on the assessments, and some folks have even taken away the numbers used to rank people. But fundamentally, we are utilizing the same accountability systems McGregor evaluated more than a half century ago.

There is no recipe or best, one-size-fits-all system for leadership accountability. At a minimum, good leaders should be able to answer the questions on the list that follows with specificity. If they can address these issues and their teams feel that they are being supported in ways that make it easier for them to make a maximum contribution, then it seems we will be making progress.

1. Does the team share a common vision of what we are trying to accomplish over the next 18 to 24 months?
2. Does the team share a common sense of present reality?
3. Do we have a plan to close the gap between present reality and what we intend to create in the future?
4. Do we have a quantifiable way to measure progress toward accomplishing our goals that allows us to track progress and celebrate improvements?
5. Do people on the team feel that they can question progress and have their voices heard?

6. How are you changing to make changes on the team more likely?
7. What are you doing to prepare yourself to lead more in the future?

We are not suggesting that these questions are exhaustive or that a leader who can address these issues will be successful. There is no substitution for leaders who care for people, are passionate about the task, and are curious learners. What we are suggesting, is that very few leaders we have met can answer most of these questions effectively. We are suggesting that if they can't articulate a future vision, haven't created a shared sense of reality, or don't have a plan, their chances at success are limited.

We're advocating that, as leaders, we shed the shackles of past systems that give a false sense of accountability and don't challenge us to evaluate the most basic questions facing our teams. It's time that we stop creating the eighth edition of what didn't work last year and find a better, more effective way to help leaders develop and become more accountable in the future.

A Good Place to Start—Fifty Years in the Making

Before he died in 1970, Abe Maslow, the father of humanistic psychology, set out a list of behaviors that he believed are precursors to the development of more actualized individuals willing to connect, learn, and grow.[7] The list, as amended by many who furthered his research, seems even more relevant today. Maslow's point was a simple one: If leaders can foster more of these behaviors in the cultures that they create, people will be more likely to choose to more fully engage. Most of these behaviors are, at their core, mindful expressions of a set of values that are more likely to facilitate a culture that supports engagement and creative expression.

To Maslow's point, these behaviors are rarely supported in most cultures. It is far more common for organizational cultures to value behaviors that provide an illusion of certainty, promote individual gain over teamwork and comfort over honesty, and 'getting along' over challenging the status quo. To build a culture that supports being different and learning to love weird ideas, we must learn to act on a different set of values, even when these behaviors increase our discomfort level significantly. For most, building cultures that support these behaviors will require a dramatic shift in the way we think about effective leadership and successful performance. It won't be easy. It will take time. Shouldn't we all be accountable for supporting people who:

1. Mindfully experience life like a child, full of absorption and wonder?
2. Try new things instead of sticking to the safe path?

3. Listen to their own feelings in evaluating experiences; resist giving in to the pressures of tradition or the opinions of the majority of those in authority?
4. Avoid inauthenticity and game-playing?
5. Are honest even when it is difficult?
6. Are prepared to be unpopular when their views are in the minority?
7. Take responsibility, especially when things don't work out as planned?
8. Are mindful of their defenses and have the courage to give them up even when it is risky?

Chapter 5 | Summary

1. Accountability must not be solely the responsibility of leaders. On the best teams, accountability is mutual. It's a promise that every member of the team makes to do their best and to ensure that others do the same.
2. On the best teams, accountability can be harsh, even unwavering. People are expected to do their best, to keep their promises. In the best cultures, mediocrity is neither sought nor tolerated.
3. The role of the leader is to ensure a constant state of creative tension. The leader must ensure that people have a shared sense of reality and a vivid picture of what the team intends to create. This tension can create a sense of urgency for change. Wearing rose-colored glasses and pretending that things are better than they are will not make a team more positive or more motivated. Rather, it will rob the team of a shared understanding of the challenges faced in attempting to build momentum and alter the course of team performance.
4. Core values are not core to the team if they are not supported by the commitment of all team members.
5. Structuring accountability into "the way we do our work" is a way of ensuring that we don't fall victim to the tendency to avoid the discomfort that comes from seeing the world the way it is and not the way we wish it were.
6. Accountability has been too focused on improvement relative to last year's or last week's performance. Although important, focusing on improvements relative

to past actions can lead to chronic underperformance. If we are to be accountable for giving our best, we must learn to compare today's performance with our potential. Better than yesterday isn't saying much when we are capable of extraordinary.

7. At a minimum, leaders must be accountable for developing:
    a. A clear and compelling description of the intended future.
    b. A shared understanding of present performance.
    c. A plan for leading people to take responsibility for closing the gap between A and B.
    d. A feedback process to measure progress.
    e. A plan for improving their abilities as a leader to engage people in pursuit of the common cause.

Learn to Love Different

Here's to the crazy ones / The misfits / The rebels / The troublemakers / The round pegs in the square holes / The ones who see things differently / They are not fond of rules / And they have no respect for the status quo / You can quote them / Disagree with them / Glorify or vilify them / About the only thing you can't do is ignore them / Because they change things / They push the human race forward / And while some may see them as the crazy ones / We see Genius / Because the people who are crazy enough to think they can change the world, / Are the ones that do.

This is a transcript of an Apple commercial known as 'The Crazy Ones.' The ad won the 1998 Emmy Award for best commercial and, as part of Apple's Think Different campaign, helped the company reverse its trajectory in the marketplace. This iconic commercial narrated by actor Richard Dreyfuss resonated, at least in part, because it was an emotional representation of what most of us believe to be true. To change the world, we must be willing to love differently, think differently, believe differently, and act differently. If we are not willing to challenge the status quo today, we cannot expect to create substantially different results tomorrow.

However, as much as we revere those who dare to be different and praise the brave, creative souls who have changed the world, empirical research and our own experience show that our espoused love of misfits, rebels, and troublemakers may not be as universal as our words suggest. Although we admire creativity and being different in theory, most of us have an inherent bias for the status quo that causes us to dismiss creative ideas. Consequently, different ideas, thoughts, backgrounds, and ways of doing things are far more likely to be rejected than valued in most cultures. Too often, we like to talk about the value of being an innovative "wild duck," but then turn around in the next breath and punish the expression of the very ideas that we say we admire. This is as true today as it has always been.

History has not been kind to the most creative and innovative among us. The leaders and trailblazers we most admire were often ridiculed, tortured, and fitted with unflattering labels. The Roman Inquisition imprisoned Galileo until he died for expressing his theory that the earth and other planets in our solar system rotated around the sun. Martin Luther King Jr. was labeled a troublemaker before being recognized as one of the most influential leaders in American history. Ted Turner was widely mocked as he pitched the concept of a 24-hour news channel. Top executives at NBC initially rejected the show Seinfeld, reasoning that it was "too New York and too Jewish" to be accepted by national audiences. The American writer Ralph Waldo Emerson had it right in 1841 when he warned that the world conspires to get people to conform.

To be successful in the future, we will have to recognize our differences as a source of advantage. We will have to overcome our inclination to pull the familiar close and to push the unfamiliar away. We will have to embrace diversity in all forms, because diversity is a prerequisite to learning, creativity, and innovation. It will require that we build a process that can withstand people's natural resistance to change. A brief history of the development of the Crazy Ones Commercial can be instructive in this regard.

Steve Jobs had just been rehired as the CEO of Apple Computer. He soon realized that the company was in worse shape than he had anticipated, and believed that the brand needed to be refreshed. To assist in the company makeover, Jobs called on Chiat/Day (CD), a marketing firm based in Venice Beach, Calif.[1] (Ironically, they had been fired ten years earlier from the account.) At their initial meeting, Jobs made it clear that he did not want a transformational campaign. He wanted to start small and grow the marketing campaign as Apple customers began to see that the company was changing.

The CD team had different ideas. In their first meeting, its members convinced Jobs to abandon his plan to start small and to embrace a bolder and more significant rebranding effort. The initial excitement of the CD and Apple teams hit a wall months later when the Crazy Ones initial concept-video was played for Jobs. His response was "It sucks! I hate it! It's advertising agency shit! I thought you were going to write something like 'Dead Poets Society' This is crap!"

The CD team was shocked. They believed in the Crazy Ones concept. Why was it crap? Was the video too emotional? Not different enough? Not what Steve Jobs was expecting? It's still unclear what Jobs didn't like about the video, but his draconian response was demoralizing. The team could have quit. Some of them did. But the core of the team loved the concept and persisted through the frustrations, disagreements, and anxiety-provoking conversations in spite of Jobs' reaction. After exploring alternative directions for several weeks, the team finally embraced a version of the advertisement that was markedly similar to the concept video he initially rebuked. The team, including Jobs, had come full circle. What had been dismissed as "crap" was about to become an Emmy-winning commercial. Both teams found a way to grow comfortable with the discomfort that is the creative process.

The culture that characterized much of the CD-Apple partnership in the creation of the Crazy Ones reflected the creativity inherent in a diverse and talented team. It was also illustrative of the conflict that is inevitable when talented people have their strongly held beliefs questioned. There were heated disagreements. People were uncomfortable. People quit and then rejoined the team. By almost all accounts, the creative tension in this process was typical of the experience of most teams when people's beliefs are challenged directly.

Most of us are creatures of habit who prefer certainty, who like to feel in control, and who have a history of being rewarded for having the answers. It should not be a surprise that so many of us have well-developed defensive routines that protect us from the inevitable discomfort that results when we work to capture the advantages inherent in our diverse backgrounds and experiences. As the commercial infers, for many, it is easier to label those who appear different as the Crazy Ones, the misfits, the rebels, or the troublemakers than to allow their ideas to challenge our beliefs.

Learn to Love Weird Ideas

In the Crazy Ones commercial, the people pictured as Richard Dreyfuss read the script—Albert Einstein, John Lennon, Mohammed Ali, Pablo Picasso and others—were icons of the 20th century. Their likenesses gave the ad power. Most of us, however, will never have the privilege of having the next Einstein challenge our thinking. Most of the people who will challenge us will be far less famous. When they bring us a creative idea, it will often come disguised as the crazy idea of a person who just doesn't get it. But some ideas that look weird or far-fetched at first glance will have the potential to change our lives. The difference between weird and brilliant can be a fine line that is rarely obvious at first.

We met Dr. Bob nearly 30 years ago at an Ohio Dental Society meeting. At the time, Bob had a modest pediatric dental practice in Westerville, Ohio, and came to the meeting to try to pick up a few 'management ideas.' We could tell from our first conversation that he was not quite like anyone we had met before. He wore his love for people on his sleeve. His desire to innovate was apparent as he described how he had just given each of the five members of his staff $1,000 to find new ways to help him build his practice.

"Do any of them have experience in building dental practices?" we asked.

"Hell no," he told us. "They are young. It's a receptionist, a tech and a couple of hygienists."

"And you gave them cash?"

"Yep. I empowered them to help me build the future."

At first we laughed and teased him about his unconventional way of marketing his practice. But we weren't laughing long.

Several months later, one of the hygienists came to work with a box containing thousands of stickers—pig stickers that read, "Dr. Bob Loves You." Dr. Bob was not happy and was quick to share his displeasure: "You're wasting my money. Pig stickers? Thousands of pig stickers? What were you thinking?"

Over the next couple of months, it turned out that moms and kids loved the stickers. They stuck them everywhere—literally everywhere. They became a part of the practice. It absolutely drove Dr. Bob crazy that he had to reorder the stickers just a couple of months later.

When he retired a few years ago, we were there to celebrate with him. He had created the largest pediatric dental practice in the Midwest. He was one of a kind. He regularly provided services to children who could not afford a dentist. Only one employee left the practice in almost 30 years. When we put him on the *Legendary Service* video years ago, the stories we heard from staff and patients had us all in tears.

When we asked him for the secret to his success, the entire staff chuckled as they looked at the wall in the building with a picture of a pig and the inscription DR. BOB LOVES YOU. He laughed as he told us that it was the dumbest idea ever, it just so happened that it worked. It worked so well that Dr. Robert Gardiner DDS is not well known, but Dr. Bob, the pig guy, is an institution.

We asked him what had resulted from the other $4,000 he gave out that day. He told us that there were some much better ideas than the stickers, but they just didn't work.

"If she had asked you for permission to buy the stickers" we asked? NFW was his response. "Thank heavens she didn't ask," he added.

Dr. Bob's story still guides our thinking when we consider how we might build a culture that captures the advantages inherent in our differences. The rough road map to such a culture can be found in the Crazy Ones commercial: someone appears with a unique perspective, be it a pig sticker or the theory of relativity. The unique ideas face inevitable resistance from defenders of the status quo. The one offering the creative idea is labeled a misfit, rebel, non-team player, or worse as he or she is pressured to conform. But the "misfit" persists, and eventually his or her ideas find resonance with a larger group and something remarkable is created as a result.

Embracing Different Can Provide a Competitive Advantage

Advocating that we learn to love different, embracing greater diversity and building stronger relationships with people who are different than we are, is not a plea borne of political correctness. It is not a suggestion that we accept our differences so that we can "get along." It is not just an argument that, as leaders, we should do the right thing, though we should. We are saying that our teams suffer when we perpetuate a worldview that encourages us to retreat to our corners and surround ourselves primarily with people from our tribes. Building high-performing, innovative teams will require that we learn to embrace every person's unique gifts. We must learn to develop relationships with people of different genders, ethnicities, experiences, educations, competencies, and beliefs because it is through their eyes that we will learn to see the world differently, to challenge existing orthodoxies, and to generate new ideas that help us create better and different futures.

The research is clear: Teams with more diversity are more innovative. The inclusion of people who think differently and believe differently can create a strategic competitive advantage. The research conducted in the last couple of years tells an unambiguous story.

In a study of more than 3,000 of the largest publicly traded companies in the United States, researchers from North Carolina State University found "that there is a causative link—it's not just a correlation" between diversity and innovation. The finding, they noted, "extends across a broad range of industry sectors."[2]

Additionally, researchers from the Boston Consulting Group explored the relationship between innovation and diversity based on gender, age, national origin, career path, industry, background, and education.[3] These researchers found a statistically significant relationship between diversity and innovation in every one of the eight countries included in the study. The more dimensions of diversity represented in the organization, the stronger the correlation. They also found that increased diversity had a significant bottom-line effect. The more diverse companies had 19 percent higher innovation revenues and 9 percent higher earnings before interest and taxes.

A McKinsey and Company study in 2017 found a similar correlation between diversity and profitability.[4] In its study of 300 multinationals, McKinsey found that companies in the top quartile of ethnic diversity are 33 percent more likely to outperform their competitors financially. An analysis of the Forbes 50 best workplaces for diversity found that these companies enjoy 24 percent higher year-over-year revenue growth than companies that do not make the list.[5] Even in the venture capital world, where diversity remains a rarity in the U.S., a 2018 study revealed that teams with greater diversity significantly improved portfolio-company returns and overall fund returns.[6]

The benefits associated with enhanced diversity may be even stronger when it comes to education. There is a large body of research extending back decades that has demonstrated that heterogeneous classrooms lead to a host of positive learning outcomes. These studies show that students in more diverse settings are better prepared for employment in the global economy, have enhanced critical thinking skills, have better-developed leadership abilities, and are more prepared for cross-cultural dialogue in a pluralistic society.

Notwithstanding the compelling evidence of the inherent value in learning to love different, most leaders and most organizations seem unwilling to fully embrace the challenge. Our collective need for comfort and certainty often continues to win out over our need to embrace different and creative ideas. Most of us love certainty more than we are willing to admit. We like when things are predictable. We seek out simple solutions. We avoid conflict-filled debates. Doing more of what we did yesterday tends to reduce our anxiety and often has the benefit of helping us "get stuff done" today. It feels good to have people agree with us. Meetings that have more agreement and less conflict are often regarded as "effectively led meetings." In many cases, it is still more career-enhancing to do the safe thing than it is to do the creative one. Creative ideas are, by definition, novel. And because many, if not most, of these ideas fail, people often have a hard time seeing novel ideas as practical. This frequently results in a knee-jerk reaction in which the most creative suggestions are dismissed as too weird, not timely, or both. We may not like to think that we run with the herd or that we let our past practices dictate our future actions, but, too often, we do.

When we advocate learning to love different, what we are advocating goes well beyond simple acceptance of diversity or increased cultural awareness. To be successful in the future, we must learn to love and not simply tolerate the things that make us different. We must learn to embrace the disruption that will inevitably result when people challenge the very things that form the foundations of past successes. We will get more comfortable with innovation only when we choose to delve into uncertain waters more frequently. When we do, we will discover that, in most cases, the learning that results will be worth the risks taken.

For most groups, learning to capture the innovative potential of our teams will require that we:

- Reinvent how information is handled.
- Make learning part of everyone's job.
- Teach everyone the rules of the game.
- Structure hiring practices to ensure a diverse and talented team.

Stop Managing Information

We have all been to "the meeting." It usually starts with a shared listing of the major challenges faced by the group. These challenges are then triaged as a means of creating a focus on near-term objectives. For the vast majority of teams, the number one issue listed is almost always "poor communication."

For most of our careers we considered 'poor communication' too broad a category to be actionable. So we pushed teams to be more specific. We urged them not to use the catch-all phrase "communication" but rather to try to identify the actual issues facing the team. We believed that teams would improve faster if they took the time to address the root causes of their challenges. We were wrong. We weren't listening.

It now seems unthinkable that it took us so long to understand what should have been obvious. Teams may have called it a communication problem, but they were telling us that they had an information problem. They were not getting the information that they needed to do their jobs. They were asking to be trusted with information that might help them better understand "the big picture." They were telling us that they were frustrated. Our attempts to get these teams to stop using the phrase "poor communications" only increased that frustration. They were suggesting that the organization rethink how information was generated, shared, and used. They were asking to be included, to be informationally connected to the rest of the team and the organization's mission.

These were simple, common-sense requests. "Give us the information so that we can do our jobs better." How could we have missed the urgency in their requests? How could it be that, in nearly every organization, so many people felt uninformed and unheard? How could so many people, including us, not realize that people were being denied relevant information even as we talked about the perils of the Information Age? And how could we so consistently have mismanaged information that we unintentionally frustrated the very people that we were trying desperately to engage?

The sad but correctable truth is that we have not been mindful of the way we have used and misused information. In the name of "management," we have unnecessarily restricted the flow of information. We have narrowed many roles to the point that we have created a dichotomy in organizations separating the "doers" from the "thinkers." In many cases, the thinkers were not that eager to share the control that comes with widely sharing information. And in the name of efficiency, we have too often felt the need to separate the important information from the "noise" so that more junior people (often the doers) in the organization would not become distracted. This management of information flow is similar to what the military would call information sharing on a "need to know" basis. And, who needs to know is almost always determined by a few thinkers in the organization whose power is solidified by restricting the flow of that information.

We are not arguing that it has been management's intent to disempower people. We are arguing that the unintended effect of many inherited management practices is to restrict or weaponize information and, in the process, significantly inhibit innovation, engagement and, inevitably, goal attainment.

A few years ago, we were discussing with hotel general managers the ways in which hotels can gather customer information in support of their service improvement efforts. At the time, most hotels provided a survey form in every guest room that requested that the guest fill out a survey and then "hand it to the front desk clerk or put it in the suggestion box" before leaving the property.

We asked the GMs in the meeting why guests could not just leave the surveys in the room and have housekeeping collect them. From their reaction, you would have thought that we had just made the dumbest suggestion ever. “That won’t work. If you leave it in the room, housekeeping will simply throw the survey away if it is negative.”

“Really? Don’t they want feedback?” we asked.

“I am not sure they want feedback, even when it is positive,” was their first response. “However, when the feedback identifies problems, I think many would simply rather avoid the survey results altogether. That’s why we suggest handing the form to a manager so that we can ensure that the customer’s suggestions become part of our improvement efforts.”

It took an hour before the group questioned their assumption that housekeepers could not be trusted with customer feedback. When they finally began to address the issue, it took only seconds for them to conclude that housekeepers didn’t fear the feedback, they feared what might be done with the feedback. They thought that employee fear of management’s reaction was overblown. However, there was nearly universal agreement that most housekeepers in their hotels were rarely asked to participate in the development of the processes in which they work. They were, as one put it, followers not leaders.

The problem with being called a follower is that, eventually, you will begin to act like a follower and expect to be treated like a follower. In the process, followers grow to be known as non-leaders and they are robbed of the energy and drive required to meaningfully participate in helping to create the future. When we manage information, we control the flow of that information in ways that tell people whether they are valued and whether their ideas will be considered.

It is probably true that most housekeepers are not punished because of customer feedback. It is also probably true that many housekeepers fear the consequences of negative survey results. But neither of these issues captures the scope of the harm that is done when information is 'managed' in ways that limit people's willingness and ability to lead—regardless of job description.

To create an environment that is conducive to learning and innovation, we need to stop managing information. Managing information in the sense of planning, organizing, and controlling it is nonsensical. In a world where information is ubiquitous, where the need for innovation is apparent, and where we expect every person regardless of position to participate in the creation of the future, everyone must be willing to lead and information must be widely shared.

In the future, we must make the way we collect and share information a strategic consideration. Widely shared information is the lifeblood of an organization. When it flows freely through our organizational veins, it becomes the foundation of learning and renewal. An idea is communicated. It meets a different perspective, and it becomes two ideas. Then two ideas become six and they continue to multiply. The expanding ideas and information serve to challenge the organization to put these ideas into context, to experiment with them, and eventually to put the best ones into action. At that point, information ceases to be "bits of data" and becomes the fuel that energizes and focuses people's efforts to create a future that, as management consultant Peter Drucker liked to say, can be seen but is not yet visible.

Learning Must Be Everyone's Responsibility

Diverse information is of little value if we don't learn from it. The best leaders are naturally curious. They have a high question-to-statement ratio and an enduring belief that they have something to learn from everyone. They seek diverse opinions because they understand that until someone challenges their point of view, their thinking is just rearranging their prejudices. For them, learning is not just assimilating facts or memorizing the answers to problems that were solved yesterday; it is a process of discovery that is enhanced by the levels of diversity on the team. The best leaders understand that discovering new and different courses of action will require that they embrace a diversity of viewpoints while looking reality squarely in the eye.

Despite the precedents set by exemplary leaders and the decades-old movement advocating the creation of "learning organizations," it's stunning how frequently many of us underestimate the challenges inherent in embracing ideas that accelerate learning. Our belief that learning is natural and energizing is understandable but often unrealistic. For many, learning something new, especially if the new information disproves an old belief, can create significant anxiety.

Learning was much easier when we were kids. When we were young, we needed to learn, walk, eat, talk, and interact with our external environment. We acted with less fear. When trying new things, if we didn't succeed at first, we persisted. Failure was no big deal, and we were not embarrassed when we changed tactics. The people around us celebrated our every step, literally. They supported our gurgled utterances and pretended that we said their names. Tomorrow needed to be different. So, we learned to learn; it was natural.

But then life happened. We were socialized into the ways of the world. We went to school and were quickly taught that it was important to conform even if it lessened our curiosity. We learned that being different was not always safe. We tried out for the sports team, band, or school play, and discovered that our chances for success were better when we conformed to rules and group norms.

Then we went to work. There we learned that appearing smart and having an answer, even if it was not the right answer, was often highly rewarded. We also discovered that challenging present practices could be threatening, even embarrassing. This is especially true in cultures that reward the all-stars, the people who always seem to have the answers.

The result of this socialization process was that we learned the perils involved in being different and embracing different points of view. Predictably, creative problem solving often took a back seat to "getting along" and "not creating waves." We became experts in deflection and the development of rational defensive routines. Political behavior won out over curious inquiry. Over time, many of us learned to develop what Stanford professor Carol Dwek calls a "fixed mindset," one in which proving to those around us that we are competent becomes more of a priority than actually learning to be competent.[7]

Some were able to swim against the tide, to resist the many pressures to conform. Their natural curiosity flourished. They retained what some call a learning or growth mindset. They remained willing to take risks and dive into the deep end of the pool before people thought that they were ready. They believed that they would figure out how to swim once they were in the water. Importantly, these people knew they didn't have all the answers to their challenges, and consistently sought the advice and input of others as they strove to build competence. As this group of non-conformists tasted greater levels of success, their ability to learn allowed them to attack the unknown faster and more creatively. The best, those that we admire and write about, not only remained curious in the face of pressures to conform, but also learned to create cultures in which others were more likely to do the same.

The Total Quality Movement in North America was also, at its heart, a learning movement. When it began, most companies were an order of magnitude removed from world-class quality metrics. It wasn't until frontline teams became responsible for using statistical process control to reduce variation that the approach to quality began to change. Call it TQM or Lean or Agile, the systematic reduction of variation was the result of engaging people who previously had been shielded from information and schooled to follow the rules. Now this same group was transforming manufacturing as they reviewed complex data sets and transformed into teams of responsible learners.

Great athletic coaches don't just review the stats that describe yesterday's performance. They routinely ask their players what they learned. These coaches know that athletes must "learn how to learn" more effectively. They must become their own best coaches in order to be optimally prepared for success in competition. Exceptional classroom teachers don't ask, "What will I teach today?" Instead, they ask, "What will students learn today?" For them, success is always defined by the level of student learning.

Curious leaders encourage learning naturally. They can't help it. It is part of who they are. The rest of us (which is most of us), who have been more heavily influenced by environmental and social pressures, must become avid learners before we can expect others to do the same. If we are not authentically curious in seeking and appreciating diverse views, and if we are not willing to confront our own beliefs, we can't expect others to follow.

Maybe the greatest challenge to learning is overcoming the effects of our past success. Researchers have shown that the most successful among us often have atrophied learning muscles. Investigators have concluded that because we learn more from our failures than our successes, and because most cultures reward success and punish failures, many successful leaders may not have failed enough to grow their ability to learn. They've succeeded by having the best answers, so why should they change now? Unfortunately, when leaders become less curious, less likely to explore, and less likely to embrace different points of view, their beliefs quickly spread like a viral cultural message throughout the organization. Faster than we believe possible, an organizational learning disability becomes ingrained in our culture, and team learning, innovation, and adaptability suffer predictably.

This organizational transformation will not happen until we make every person and every team responsible for learning, just as athletes learn to be in charge of their own development.

Learning must become less teacher- and boss-directed and more a natural consequence of our innate curiosity. The fear of failure will be reduced as we focus more on what we learned and how that learning informed our thinking. As we become more willing to tackle bigger problems that defy easy answers, it will become more necessary to seek the help of others, realizing that we learn best when the diversity of our teams pushes us to consider things that might not otherwise have even entered our field of vision.

Ensure Everyone Understands the Rules of the Game

"For every dollar that customers spend in our restaurant, how much profit do we make?" We asked this question to the wait staff and short-order cooks of a national restaurant company. Based on past experience, we were not surprised that the profit margin was consistently overestimated by just about everyone we interviewed. The average response: 50 cents. The workers believed, on average, that 50 cents of every dollar spent by customers ended up in the owner's pocket as profit.

The fact that employees would so consistently overestimate the profit margins of their businesses drove many restaurant managers orbital. One, in Lafayette Louisiana, lost his cool completely. "50?! Why 50?! We make 5 percent, not 50 percent," he told the group after the short-order cook had missed the mark so wildly.

The short-order cook in this restaurant could not contain himself. "You mean to tell me that if I throw this $3 piece of meat away, you have to sell $60 worth of food to make up for it?" he asked. The manager eventually got the math right and told the group that the cook was correct. The cook responded by sharing with the group that he felt sorry for people in the business who would work weekends for 5 percent.

In this restaurant, as we had seen in so many others, when the entire team wrestled with the information highlighted in the challenges inherent in running a restaurant, things changed. For the first time, many employees began to understand that making a profit in the industry was no small feat. They discussed at length how their actions affected profitability. Armed with a greater understanding of financial realities, they took more responsibility. Food costs went down significantly in most stores, and guest service increased. The short-order cook in Louisiana summed up our experience best when he told us, "Once we understood how hard it was to make money, we couldn't act the same way ever again."

We have had similar experiences in the trucking industry, in sporting goods, in the airline and automobile industries, in supermarkets, in children's apparel, and in banking. In nearly all cases, people tend to overestimate the amount of money their employer makes and tend to behave differently when they better understand the business realities faced by the company.

Maybe the best long-term example of what can happen when people inside businesses understand the rules of that business is that of Springfield Remanufacturing Corporation (SRC).[8]

SRC was a subsidiary of International Harvester. SRC rebuilt engines for Harvester. In the wake of an economic downturn, rather than shut down the factory or sell the assets, the parent company opted to sell the subsidiary to an SRC employee group in 1983.[9]

Plant manager Jack Stack, who became CEO after the purchase was finalized, was a believer in the potential of ordinary people to do extraordinary things. He was an evangelist for the proposition that every employee, regardless of position, must become financially literate. So it was not surprising that the SRC team began its new journey by learning the realities of the deal that it had made. Jack called it "open book management." It was an educational process that helped every person better understand the realities of their business so that they might better contribute to creating the future of SRC. Stack's description of the philosophy was as simple as it was profound:

> *Don't use information to intimidate, control, or manipulate people. Use it to teach people how to work together, achieve common goals, and thereby gain control over their lives... cost control happens on the level of the individual. You don't become the least-cost producer by issuing edicts from*

an office... The best way to control costs is to enlist everyone in the effort. That means providing people with the tools that allow them to make the right decisions.

When you trace SRC's history over the last 35 years, the company is more than a successful case study. It is a living reminder of what a group of diverse people can do when they get the information necessary to do their jobs, and when they understand how to play the game. In 1983, Jack and 12 other employees agreed to buy the company for $8.9 million. They put down $100,000 of their own money and assumed $8.9 million in debt. The initial stock price was 10 cents a share with annual revenues of $13 million.

Today, the company offers remanufactured components for automobiles, commercial trucks, agricultural equipment, and construction vehicles. It provides its products and services through dealers in the United States and internationally. What started as a venture to save 119 jobs that were certain to be laid off by Harvester now employs more than 1,600 people working in 17 business units, occupying over a million and a half square feet of manufacturing and warehouse space. Revenues now exceed $400 million annually, and the latest quoted stock price is $102 per share. Maybe more notably, the education of the SRC workforce has resulted in the funding of 60 companies that were born from its workforce's ideas.

Over the last four decades, our experience reinforces Stack's experience at SRC. When people understand the rules of the game and they understand how the game is played, they play better. The famous line from SAS's Jan Carlzon still rings true: "People without information cannot take responsibility. People with information can hardly help but take responsibility."[10]

Structure Competent Diversity into the Hiring Process

A few years ago, we were asked to help a market leader that was intent on changing its culture to be more creative and innovative. (Aren't we all?) The company was spending a million dollars on messaging and holding meetings with employees to help "get the word out" and to create excitement for a new culture-change initiative. But even as its leaders spoke eloquently about the need to change—even hiring a "guru" to guide their efforts—few process changes were made, and they were hesitant to reconsider the kind of people they hired on their teams. They talked of needing people who were "cultural fits" even as they held meetings in which they touted the need for disruption and cultural change.

The hiring practices that company leaders employed were similar to many that we have experienced in other organizations with similar goals. After candidates were identified, an internal team of "high-performers," along with HR representatives, reviewed the resumes of applicants to ensure that they had the requisite experience. Unfortunately, that meant that most of the applicant's' experiences were similar. The unintended result was a candidate pool with little experiential diversity.

Subsequently, the "qualified" candidates interviewed with the hiring teams after which they were ranked by the group. If any members of the hiring team had a concern about a person, the concerns were noted. Strong objections by a couple of members of the group, as a practical matter, were enough to disqualify the candidate.

Predictably, the least objectionable candidate, and typically the one who looked, acted, and thought like other members of the group, became the team's preferred choice. Vetting candidates by consensus had the unintentional effect of reducing diversity and thereby ensuring that substantial change in the organization would remain illusory. The unstated but unmistakable requirement of consensus in this organization's hiring practices all but ensured that the successful candidate would not be disruptive to the culture that the team said it wanted to disrupt.

When we asked the hiring team how the hiring process supported its espoused desire to build a culture more supportive of innovation, team members told us that their hiring criteria included experience in helping organizations change.

They said they were looking for change agents who were "experienced, smart, values-driven, collaborative people who were a cultural fit."

Pushing back, we asked them to consider different sets of characteristics of people who might be likely to help an organization change or to contribute different, creative ideas. For instance, had they valued people who were:

- Diverse in race, ethnicity, and background?
- Rarely satisfied with the status quo?
- Impatient and not always willing to take 'NO' for an answer without significant debate?
- Disruptive, at times disagreeable, and willing to question authority?
- Not easily managed?
- At times slow and hesitant to make decisions based on what we did last year? (Creativity is a slow activity)
- Unwilling to go along just to get along?

Their response neatly framed their hiring challenges:

> *Why would we hire a person who is hard to manage and is never satisfied and is always questioning what we do? We are pretty good here, you know. If we hired people who we knew would consistently challenge what we learned yesterday, we would never get anything done.*

Yes, we say we want different. We want creative. We say we want to change. We say that we need different, but do we honestly believe it? The truth is that even if we are committed to recruiting more diverse teams, we are often painfully unaware of how our hiring processes give preference to people who are more like us. As a result, we often allow the long-term effects of our biases, knowingly or unknowingly, to be hidden in our collective consciousness, in our culture. Over time, groups that cling to such processes tend to become more homogeneous, not less.

Recruiting a more diverse team begins with intention. The kind of intention required is more than a desire or wish. It is a conscious, mindful choice based on a belief that diversity is critical to the team's success. It will require that we create a process that is built with the need for diversity in mind. Our preference for people who look and think and act like us is strong and can only be overcome with a structured commitment to embrace people who often make us uncomfortable.

When the show "Full Frontal with Samantha Bee" was staffing up, hiring writers for the political satire, Jo Miller, the showrunner at the time, used an evaluation for screening writers that was similar to the ones used on other sitcoms. However, Miller added some tweaks to ensure that past biases were minimized.[11] The hiring team wanted to ensure that the more superficial parts of a person's bio did not outweigh the applicant's talent or potential. The team implemented a blind submissions process—no names were attached to writers' applications. This made it easier for industry outsiders to submit their work. The submission packet was templated in ways that ensured that Bee, Miller, and others couldn't tell if the applicant was a comedy pro, a new college grad, or a 45-year-old making a career change.

The show had created a process in which the people judging the applications were not allowed to 'see' the applicants when initially judging their competence. They wanted competent and diverse, and by not allowing their biases to limit their perception of competence, they were able to identify more qualified candidates. After ensuring that the candidates were qualified, the hiring team made diversity a significant factor in the process. They believed that a diverse team, one that looked more like their viewers, would create more entertaining scripts. They were right. The cohort of writers that was eventually hired was not only talented but also diverse. Half of the group were women, and 30 percent were people of color. The moral of this story is that if we are truly committed to hiring a diverse and competent team, we can do so—especially if we create structures to help us overcome our biases.

If we look closely, we will see that many of our present hiring practices are designed in ways that limit the number of "different" people who get invited to join. We may not be conscious of our bias, but most people are simply more comfortable with the familiar. It's not that we don't value diversity, don't want to change, or don't want our ideas questioned. Often, it is because we have become unwitting prisoners of the existing culture. The unrealized and unarticulated pressures in some cultures can lead us to develop processes with the best of intentions, yet, remain blind to the fact that many of these processes undermine our espoused intention to learn to embrace our differences.

Some ideas:

1. Start early. It's easier to become diverse before biases have become ingrained in our hiring practices.
2. Be clear on the type of people you hope to hire. Share your values? Competent? Good thinker? Willing to change? Willing to speak truth to power? Confident? Good leader? Having clarity as to our intentions is a necessary first step to building a successful hiring process.
3. Put more diversity, of all types, on your hiring team. The research is clear that a diverse hiring team will recruit more diverse members for our teams.
4. Expand your personal and professional networks. Our personal preferences are affected by our experiences. For example, research shows that fathers with daughters are more likely to hire women. Having more experience with an unrepresented group makes their inclusion more likely.
5. Confront bias when you see it. When we tolerate bias, we teach that bias is acceptable.

Chapter 6 | Summary

1. Learning to appreciate our differences is a potential source of significant competitive advantage. Only when people challenge us to think and act differently can we create anything remarkable.
2. In most cases, people are hesitant to embrace different ideas, especially when they undermine our past beliefs. We have many well-developed defensive routines that tend to inhibit a group's ability to fully consider the potential of different ideas offered by different people.
3. We like stability and certainty and simplicity. Different ideas can make us uncomfortable. Too often, the discomfort that we feel is allowed to undermine the creative process.
4. Learning should be part of everyone's job. We've never seen a person who is actively learning and turned off. We have seen many brilliant people become bored and disengaged.
5. Information is the lifeblood of an effective organization. Information should not be managed. In today's world, it must be allowed to flow freely throughout.
6. Information without a context for understanding and acting on that information is just data. Teach everyone the business. Make sure they understand the rules of the game. Only then can they capture the advantages of diverse information.

7. Learning is not all fun and games. Learning creates anxiety. And most people won't embrace learning outside the confines of a psychologically safe environment.
8. If we are serious about becoming more diverse, we will have to structure diversity into the hiring process. Diversity should not be the only criteria for recruitment, but it should be an important goal of every team to have enough diversity to match or exceed the diversity of its competitive environment.

Seek Commitment, Not Compliance

"There are two ways of being creative. One can sing and dance. Or one can create an environment in which singers and dancers flourish."
— *Warren Bennis*

"Half the leaders that I have met don't need to learn what to do. They need to learn what to stop doing."
— *Peter Drucker*

"The key question isn't 'What fosters creativity?' But why in God's name isn't everyone creative? Where was the human potential lost? How was it crippled? I think therefore a good question might not be why do people create? But why do people not create or innovate?"
— *Abraham Maslow*

It has been one of the pre-eminent motivational challenges of every era since the discovery of broccoli. How can parents motivate kids to eat their vegetables? We all want healthy children and believe that eating greens is a giant step in the right direction. Yet, however logical or noble the pursuit, it has been a tough lift for many. Pizza, chicken nuggets, and French fries are all tastier than broccoli, leaving these mini-trees as the lone survivors on many dinner plates.

To get children to eat their vegetables, we have often tried to provide them with a little extra incentive, often borrowing ideas that our parents used with us. True to our past, we have often offered an "if you do this, you will get that" incentive. If you eat your broccoli, you'll get to eat dessert, to watch TV, to hang out with friends, or to play video games.

At first blush, many of these vegetable incentive systems seem to work. When the reward is attractive enough, it moves kids—it moves them to get the reward. It does not, however, move them to love broccoli.

These incentives were designed to get compliance, to get children to eat vegetables. In retrospect, the incentives may not have done that as effectively as we might have hoped.

These rewards caused some of us to learn the covert art of undetected food removal. To earn that extra TV time or after-dinner ice cream, we cultivated creative, highly advanced techniques. Some of us slyly hid our broccoli in our laps 'till after dinner. The bolder among us mastered the ability to appear to be consuming the veggies, only to later cough them into a napkin, which would then be either shuffled into the trash can or secretly flushed without detection. In most cases, we not only didn't learn to love vegetables, but we also resisted eating them by any means possible. The entire process seemed to reinforce the belief that vegetables must not be very tasty. After all, "They don't bribe us to eat the pizza or to finish the ice cream sundae."

This is a simple, silly example. But we chose it to begin this chapter because it demonstrates the ubiquity of the use of incentives in our culture. Incentives touch nearly every part of our lives, classroom to boardroom. Incentives are tactics taken from the same playbook as the grades that teachers employ to ensure kids work hard in school. Sales managers have become so reliant on these schemes that they have a hard time imagining a future without performance-based incentives. As the chairman of several public Compensation Committees, there was always a small army of consultants willing, for a fee, to tell us the best way to use incentives to get better executive performance. Yet another group of consultants was willing, for an even larger fee, to tell us how we should organize those incentives to satisfy shareholders.

Our belief in the effectiveness of incentives has become so accepted that we rarely question their effectiveness. If we question them at all, we question whether the reward is big enough or whether what is required to get the reward is clearly articulated and achievable. It has become HR wisdom that incentives are an effective way to teach students, motivate workers, and raise children.

But a half-century of research demonstrates that our belief in the effectiveness of incentives may be seriously misplaced.[1] Expecting incentives to result in employee engagement is like expecting an ice cream sundae to get our kids to love veggies. It's not going to happen. Engaging people emotionally will require us to more fully examine our relationship with incentives. It will require that we become more mindful of the unintended effects of using extrinsic, manipulative rewards. And it will require that we find a way of engaging people that is more consistent with what the behavioral sciences have taught us over the last half-century about why some people make commitments to causes—and why others resist.

Stop the Motivational Insanity

Einstein was reported to have said that insanity is doing the same thing over and over again and expecting a different result. If that is true, then many of us have become motivationally insane. We continue to rely heavily on the manipulation of rewards and punishments to control behavior while expecting these carrots and sticks to increase creativity, commitment, and engagement. Although the use of manipulative rewards may be the fastest and surest way to gain compliance, nearly three-quarters of a century of research in the fields of psychology, education, and business show us that the use of performance-contingent rewards tends to inhibit engagement. The research demonstrates that incentives can decrease interest, reduce intrinsic motivation, impede learning, inhibit creativity, undermine relationships, and invite unethical conduct.

The evidence of the unintended effects of our 'incentive insanity' surrounds us. In nearly every case, the incentives reduce the quality of the performance that they were designed to support. Car companies hoping to increase customer satisfaction have tied rewards to customer satisfaction survey results. Anyone who has bought a car has felt the salesperson's angst as they put on the pressure to give them better marks on the JD Power survey. Sales professionals who should be focusing on customer needs have had their attention redirected as they become focused on getting the incentive, or avoiding the kick in the pants, by any means possible. As one person told us, "Look, I need all '5s' on the survey. If I don't get them, it affects my pay. This is my report card. If you have issues with the service, please don't put them on the survey." The salesperson is not confused about priorities. For him, the survey result is more important than your feedback.

The unintended effects of the No Child Left Behind law passed at the request of President George W. Bush are easy to see in retrospect. The intention of the law was to improve education by increasing school and teacher accountability. Rewarding teachers who help children learn better might have seemed like a good idea in theory, but it became less effective when teachers were incentivized based on the results of student test scores. The unintended effect of these 'teacher accountability' efforts was an increased focus on test scores. Predictably, teacher creativity, teacher engagement, and student learning suffered as many teachers 'taught to the test.'

The negative impact of rewards and learning are most apparent when we begin to analyze the impact grades have on student commitment to learning. As guest lecturers in a behavioral economics class at a local university, we were recently confronted with the unintended effects of our addiction to incentives that come disguised as grades. We were surprised when our first question was met with a question. Before we could frame the discussion, a student interrupted and asked if "this material was going to be on the test?" She went on to explain that she only has time to pay attention to information that will be on the test. "How about learning something new?" we asked.

"That would be nice," she said. "I just don't have the time."

"Don't have the time to learn? You or your parents are spending more than $50,000 a year just on tuition . . ."

She interrupted us. "My job here is to get good grades so I can get into grad school. That's why my parents sent me here."

Even she laughed when we made a smart-ass remark about the possibility of buying grades for much less than fifty grand. The timing of her question caught us by surprise, but the sentiment underlying her question was far less surprising.

Students have been telling us for years that getting an 'A' in class is far more important for many than actually learning the coursework. When we asked this group to choose between taking a tough class in which the opportunity for learning would be high and good grades more difficult to get and taking a class in which opportunities to learn would be low but A's easier to get, the answers were predictable and deflating. The vast majority of the class chose the easy, even if expensive, A. The reward had become more important than learning. When we discussed our experiences with college administrators and professors, their reactions were equally deflating. No one seemed to be the least bit surprised and no one seemed to have much of an appetite to change these processes. One professor seemed to say what others were thinking: "If we didn't grade students, most of them would never come to class."

"Even if the class was interesting," we asked? They just shook their heads convinced that we just didn't get it.

We don't want to beat a dead horse, but it is important that we become more aware of how prevalent our reliance on extrinsic incentives has become and how devastating these systems can be to engagement. Even a cursory review of the research leads to the inevitable conclusion that our addiction to, and affinity for, "if you do this, you will get that" incentive systems should be significantly reduced or eliminated. In a meta-analysis of 128 individual experimental studies on the research of extrinsic vs. intrinsic motivation, Drs. Deci and Ryan of the University of Rochester and Dr. Koestner of McGill University concluded that incentivized rewards tend to have a substantial negative effect on intrinsic motivation, the motivation that exists when the task is its own reward.[2] Additionally, these studies provide evidence that, of all the different incentive schemes, the most damaging to intrinsic motivation are the ones contingent on performance. We don't know of a single peer-reviewed study that shows that the use of extrinsic rewards furthers engagement or creative thought. There is, however, a significant body of research that shows that incentives often:

> ***Decrease interest and intrinsic motivation****—Manipulative incentives change the way we think about the challenges we face. They can make things that we used to do for fun feel like work. It may seem counter-intuitive, but a long line of experiments has shown that extrinsic incentives often result in less commitment and lower-quality work.*
>
> ***Impede learning and creativity****—The negative effects of performance-based incentives are most likely felt when the task requires learning, collaboration, and creativity. Creativity requires that we work in the present, not concerned with what happened yesterday or what might happen tomorrow. Incentives do just the opposite. They get us to focus on the future reward at the expense of the present challenge.*
>
> ***Inhibits change****—It seems like common sense. When we want people to change, to learn, or to experiment with better methods, we need people who are willing to make a few*

mistakes in search of a better, different way forward. But when we are chasing a reward, there is a tendency to rely on experience and to take the path that is most certain, the one that worked for us yesterday. Unintentionally, incentives tend to anchor us in past practices.

***Undermines relationships**—When a group is vying for a reward and only a limited number of people can win, they compete. That's the game that was set up. That's the game they will play. It's commonly believed that this kind of competition will lead to increased performance, but usually it doesn't. More often, it exaggerates power differences, undermines people's willingness to share information, and destroys trust.*

***Invites unethical behavior**—What are people willing to do to get a big bonus? Or to get an A in the class? Or to get a better performance review than their peers? The research confirms what we already know. People are willing to do whatever it takes. Fabricate sales? Cheat on the test? Fudge the numbers? Undermine peers? Depending on the size and desirability of the reward or the severity of the consequences for non-performance, many people will try to find a shortcut, ethics notwithstanding.*[3]

The research has been consistent for a long time, but so has our collective desire for the sense of control that incentives provide. That illusion of control, however, comes at a price that, in most cases, remains hidden because the use of manipulative incentives has become so common in everything from sales to getting kids to eat their vegetables that we no longer even question the efficacy of their use. We like author and educator Alfie Kohn's phrasing when he challenged us to see that we have become motivationally insane:

> *There is a time to admire the grace and persuasive power of an influential idea, and there is a time to fear its hold over us. The time to worry is when the idea is so widely shared that we no longer even notice it, when it is so deeply rooted that it feels to us like plain common sense. At this point when the objections are not answered anymore because they are no longer even raised, we are not in control: we do not have the idea; it has us. (p. 3)*

But if You Take Away My Carrots and Sticks...

But if you take away 'my carrots and sticks' what tools do I have left? Unfortunately, this question, implicitly or explicitly, surfaces in nearly every conversation when people begin to rethink their dependence on extrinsic incentives. We understand the skepticism. For many, it is hard to conceptualize an organization devoid of incentives. Their belief in the power of 'carrots' has become a fundamental tenet of their leadership identity. Identities are hard to change. This is especially true when people feel that incentives have worked for them in the past and when they think that they have social proof of their effectiveness. We hear it all the time: "If incentives are ineffective, why are they so prevalent?"

We get it. They are prevalent because they give leaders a sense of control; they are easy to design, simple to implement, and the results are easy to recognize. We love simple. Deep down, we would rather avoid unnecessary complexity and we are not in a hurry to change. We don't want to give up the tools that we know will work before we are certain that there is a better way forward. So we continue to search for the better incentive plan, hoping that the next one—will be THE ONE—the one that will finally work. Predictably, most fail. They don't fail because the rewards are insufficient or because the goals are unclear. They fail because the fundamental premise of these processes are manipulative, disempowering, and distracting.

We are not naive. We don't believe that people will give up their carrots and sticks cold turkey. For decades, we have seen the disbelief in people's eyes when they are made aware of research that outlines the negative effects of reward manipulation. After reviewing some of the research, one CEO unabashedly told us, "I don't believe that stuff. It's not the real world. I know incentives work. People will work hard to get their bonuses. Bonuses have worked for me my entire career. They motivate people. That's all there is to it."

He is not an outlier. Today, many share his beliefs because these incentive processes are what they have known from the time their parents tried to get them to eat broccoli. It would be naive to expect people to jettison these processes all at once.

We do hope, however, that at a minimum, we will find a way to significantly lessen our dependence on these manipulations. We hope that we become more mindful of the fact that incentives are tools designed to gain compliance not commitment and that, in most cases, they significantly inhibit engagement. If we *can't* kick the incentive habit right away, at the very least, we must begin to design incentive processes that are less harmful to the cultures that we are trying to create. We can reduce the negative impact of "if you do this you will get that" incentives by:

- Ensuring that there are fewer incentives and that they become less important than individual and collective learning.
- Offering them as surprises for good performance and not as manipulations.
- Avoiding contests in which the number of winners is limited.
- Giving people more control over the process of how rewards are earned and distributed.

An Environment that Leads to Commitment Not Compliance

Lessening our dependence on manipulative incentives is an important first step in creating environments where people can learn and grow and where they are more willing to make an ALL-IN level of commitment. But, it is just a first step. We list it first *not* just because of the engagement-inhibiting effects of these processes. We list it first because our addiction to these processes often blinds us to fully exploring the boundaries of a different kind of motivation—a kind that can result in a passionate commitment that can keep us up at night, challenge what we believe is possible, and lead us to sacrifice for the team. It is the kind of motivation where the task is its own reward and where we lose track of time and become 'lost in the present.'

In the sections that follow, we describe ideas that we believe are critical to gaining commitment. They are not a list of steps that, if followed, will render a team committed and engaged. Rather, these sections describe actions that are critical to creating environments in which people are more willing to learn, grow, and give their best efforts. We hesitated to reduce our beliefs about creating such environments to a list for fear that it might appear that we are suggesting a simple 10-step process for gaining higher engagement. This was not our intent. Motivation and commitment naturally wax and wane even on the best of teams. Gaining commitment is a process unique to each team and requires an ongoing, concerted effort.

The following ideas are suggestions that we believe are fundamental to building highly committed, highly engaged teams.

Leaders are in the Opportunity, Not the Motivation Business

How do you motivate people? It's the question we have asked managers in executive development programs for years. The most frequent answer, by a wide margin, has been a restatement of their belief in the power of incentives coupled with an assertion that people's basic needs for security and safety must be met. It turns out that many leaders whose primary roles involve team engagement struggle to put together a cogent theory of team motivation.

MIT professor Douglas McGregor's answer to the question "How do you motivate people?" still rings true a half a century later: We don't motivate people. We can't motivate them. We don't have the power to motivate people. People are born motivated."[4] He believed that motivation is a personal choice and that the best that leaders can do is to create an environment that is so compelling that people can't wait to enlist their best efforts.

If we're serious about creating cultures that support higher levels of creativity, engagement, and commitment, the environments that we create must engage us emotionally. It's much more difficult to design a culture in which children voluntarily put vegetables on the menu, salespeople love providing service, and students love learning, than it is to design incentive systems aimed at gaining short-term compliance.

The first step in building such a culture is to *stop taking responsibility for the motivational choices of others*. Trying to motivate others is a fool's errand. It usually leads to the development of practices that place a higher value on leader control than employee engagement. The best leaders don't spend a ton of time trying to motivate others. They simply channel their inner McGregor and create environments that support people's innate need to achieve and reach their potential while ensuring that they don't do anything that would inhibit people's natural desire to contribute to a worthy cause.

To more fully engage people, leaders need to view their responsibility as providing an opportunity in which people can choose whether to be motivated—or not. People's interests are different. No job or school or team works equally well for everyone. The most we can do is create a compelling opportunity and then let people choose whether or not they want to join us in doing something remarkable.

In the Right Environment, Every Team is Capable of Commitment

We had heard about the restaurant, but we had no clue that the lunch we were attending would change us profoundly. As we entered the restaurant on the Embarcadero in San Francisco, we could sense a different energy in the room. Before we even were seated, we were looking at each other. We couldn't put our finger on why, but after just a couple of interactions with the staff, we wanted to understand what was 'motivating' them. What we were experiencing wasn't normal.

Our waiter was impeccably dressed. His enthusiasm was contagious. The food was good but good food is everywhere in San Francisco.

"You seem to really love your job?" we asked, seeking to understand the secret to the staff's engagement.

"You bet. Love this place. I am lucky to be here," he told us in a way that convinced us of his authenticity.

"Everyone seems..." We really didn't get to finish our questions before he understood that we had no idea what this place was all about.

"Delancey Street is not just the restaurant's name," he told us. "It is the name of our Foundation." He went on to explain that he and all of his teammates live and work together. He explained that he had come to Delancey Street from Oakland, California, by way of San Quentin Federal Penitentiary. He was a convicted violent felon. He explained that the remainder of the convicts-turned-employees on the restaurant team had similar backgrounds. The entire restaurant was staffed by felons, gangbangers, and drug addicts. And so, our education began.

It turned out that the Delancey Street Restaurant was just the tip of the Delancey Street iceberg. Delancey Street was a residential self-help organization for former substance abusers and violent felons. Founded in 1971 by criminologist and prison reform advocate Mimi Silbert with four people and a thousand dollars, it had grown to be recognized as a model for helping people in trouble turn their lives around.[5] The restaurant and the 370,000-square-foot housing complex were built by a 250-person workforce with no experience in construction. They were—like our waiter—ex-convicts in search of another chance at life.

Silbert liked to remind people that "most people said that it couldn't be done." She understood the skepticism. She understood the changes inherent in trying to sell the idea that a criminologist with no business experience was going to take hundreds of violent felons and multi-decade substance abusers and, with no professional counselors and no paid employees, have them build the complex, operate the restaurant, become their own therapists, and help the illiterate earn degrees. Any rational person would have more than a few doubts. But a talented person with a cause is a powerful force.

Harvard gets the top 1 percent. We recruit the bottom 1 percent. You have to be pretty bad to get in here, she once said. But with a mixture of hope, opportunity, accountability, and a belief that people learn primarily by doing, Silbert has helped the vast majority of Delancey Street residents build habits that enable them to become productive members of their communities. The Delancey Street Foundation's businesses include general contractors, (they helped build Oracle Park), truck drivers, moving companies, and furniture makers.

As we talked with our waiter that day, and with many others in the years thereafter, we began to understand why the people whom Mimi calls "the Harvard of the underclass" choose to engage. Without using either pay or manipulation, she had created an intrinsically motivated workforce. She started with a belief that people will solve their own problems. She believed that given stability, fairness, and connection, people would engage with opportunities that facilitated learning and achievement. She believed that people would "enter with a history and leave with a future" if she could create an environment that supported their natural motivations.

Our 35-year history of admiration for Mimi Silbert has not waned, even a little. Her example still gives our work direction. Delancey Street remains an unforgettable example that if the bottom 1 percent of the workforce can be intrinsically motivated to give great service, the rest of us should have few excuses. Maybe most importantly, because the team at Delancey Street refused to hire experts, and instead, gave people the opportunity to learn to solve their own challenges, it should remind us that most teams have barely scratched the surface of their potential capabilities.

The Fundamentals of a Culture that Supports Engagement

Reduce Fear. Support Relationships. Be Fair. Express Gratitude. And then, *Provide Compelling Opportunities* for people to contribute. These characteristics not only describe the Delancey Street culture, they are common to every great team we have worked with or studied. Fundamentally, these characteristics are a restatement of the work of Abe Maslow, the Father of Humanistic Psychology, who more than a half century ago transformed our thinking about how and why people are motivated. Ensure that people's basic needs are satisfied. Then provide compelling opportunities to learn, grow and create. Simple in concept. Challenging when it requires that we overcome centuries of cultural precedent.

It should not be that difficult to create high-commitment environments. If Mimi Silbert can do it at Delancey Street with violent ex-cons the rest of us should have few excuses. People want to be involved, to learn and grow. They want to be part of a cause bigger than themselves. They need strong relationships. They want to feel valued and valuable. They are simply waiting for the opportunity to be part of something remarkable. There isn't a recipe that, if followed, will create an environment that will result in higher levels of personal and group motivation. However, the outlines of a framework are clear and have been clear for decades. The following cultural attributes are consistent with what the behavioral sciences have taught us about people over the last half century and they are consistent with the best cultures that we have encountered. They are provided to help in the assessment of present cultures and in the development of cultural strategies for the future. We hope that it will help you create your own framework, one that captures your beliefs about the type of environment you believe will be required to more fully engage people and to capture the full measure of their commitment.

1. Make it safe for people to experiment. Reduce unnecessary fear.

No one wants to be fearful. We know that fear sends us to battle stations and makes us less thoughtful. Yet our addiction to using fear to control is so ingrained that we can become blind to its effects on our processes. Start with appraisal and rating practices, grades in school, and incentives. Do they unnecessarily create fear? Do we really understand the purposes of these management processes? Is there a better way of accomplishing the same things that do not generate as much fear? Are we willing to let go of some control in order to make room for others to engage?

2. Ensure an equitable environment.

We don't like to think that we act unfairly, but often we do. Most performance management systems, as currently implemented, are inherently unfair. For example, new employees are often paid more than existing employees doing the same job, making it necessary for people to leave in order to be paid fairly. Raises and bonuses are frequently based on judgments that don't mirror contribution. Do we really believe that we can rank order people fairly? Set sales quotas fairly? Do we believe that we have all the information that is required to fairly evaluate performance? Of course, some degree of unfairness is probably impossible to avoid. However, in many cases, we understand the inequity that exists but can't muster the will to change the process. We must do better. To be clear, we are not arguing that people should be treated the same. Equitable does not mean equal. It means fair. And perceived fairness is almost always a function of involvement. Cultures will nearly always be perceived as fairer when people feel that their voices have been heard.

3. Enhance everyone's ability to connect.

When we care and value each other, we see the world through a lens that allows us to build better, more trusting relationships. And because our need to connect is so fundamental to our survival and well-being, when we feel that connection, we tend to assume the best of intentions and are willing to trust more readily. Anonymity is the enemy of civility. Make sure that people get to know each other. Too often, casual conversations are viewed as wasted time. Nothing could be further from the truth. Disney's Cast Celebrations provided the opportunity for people to see the humanness in others. Few experiences were as much fun as TaylorMade Adidas Golf's Air Guitar competitions. People looked silly. People laughed. People bonded. Gymboree Idol may have been our favorite. The team grew closer as its members watched the three top executives make fools of themselves imitating American Idol judges. These events were occasions for bonding. They were investments in the building of relationships that are fundamental to a team's culture and identity.

4. Say thank you.

In four decades, we have never heard a person complain that he or she has been 'thanked' too much. We all want to be appreciated and valued. We want our commitment to be recognized. Perhaps the fastest way to enrich a culture, to make it more positive, is to thank someone. People who have been encouraged to stop, think, and express gratitude will do so without much prodding. People may not be aware of how often our competitive nature, our need for speed, and our bottom line-orientation have distracted us from basic human courtesies like saying thank you.

5. Create compelling opportunities.

Nearly every person who has been challenged to make a bigger contribution can find a way to do so successfully when given the requisite freedom, opportunity, and support. People grow by working on substantial issues. Narrowly defined job descriptions and overcontrol by management are the enemy. Involvement does not mean that you delegate all decision-making authority; it does mean that you leave space for others to participate and create. In every organization, there are a number of mind-numbing, commitment-killing practices that make it difficult for people to take responsibility for helping to create the future. We need to create a TO-STOP list that identifies these practices and eliminates them from our cultures without endless weeks of study.

6. Provide a greater opportunity to find meaning in their work.

No more dead-end jobs. Serve others. Be part of something extraordinary. We know what creates meaning for us. It won't be the same for everyone, but if we are more mindful in our conversations, we will sense when people resonate emotionally with what we are trying to do. It rarely comes from simply aiming to win the game. It almost always comes as a result of making a meaningful difference in the lives of others. Viktor

Frankl's words can serve as an important reminder: "Success, like happiness, cannot be pursued; it must ensue, and it only does so as the unintended side effect of one's personal dedication to a cause greater than oneself."[6]

What Turns Us Off is Rarely What Turns Us On

"To create a culture of creativity and innovation, we need to get serious about engagement. We talk a good game, but I feel that we are less engaged today than when we started talking about improving."

These were the words of the CEO of a technology company as they opened their strategic planning meeting a few years ago. We were asked to observe as the results of an engagement survey were distributed and discussed. The organization received high marks from employees on most of the indices of engagement that the survey attempted to measure. The results seemed to surprise no one. It was, by all accounts a caring, people-centric culture. The least positive survey results had to do with the organization's performance management process and a perceived lack of upward mobility.

To better understand how it might effectively address the engagement issues, the leadership team called a meeting and invited representatives of different parts of the organization. In analyzing the results, the group consistently focused on the survey items that received the lowest scores: performance appraisal and a lack of a clear career path. Nearly every person on the team agreed that these issues were substantially inhibiting engagement.

Over the next couple of months, group members creatively addressed both the performance appraisal and career path issues. They solicited expert advice and front-line input. The resulting implementations were a significant upgrade to the existing processes. People felt like they were making progress.

The next time the survey was administered, a year later, things had improved. Ratings for the performance management and career path scales increased dramatically. Almost across the board, people were excited by the improvements they had implemented. Despite these improvements, however, the efforts of the group had not translated into higher levels of engagement. The results of the second survey clearly showed that the number of highly engaged people had not changed, nor had the number of disengaged people decreased as a result of their efforts. The team was frustrated. The culture had improved. People felt that these improvements had made the company a better place to work. Yet, they couldn't understand why people didn't feel more engaged.

The team had assumed that if they made the work less frustrating, it would make the work more engaging. *It doesn't work that way.* The lesson the team learned is consistent with what theorists have known for more than half a century: *the things that turn us on are very different from the things that frustrate us.*

When we ask people what turns us off, most people talk about fear-inducing practices, bad relationships with peers or bosses, unfair pay, or a lack of connection or appreciation. These needs are important. When we feel a deficit in any one of these needs, it becomes prepotent; it preoccupies our attention until the need is addressed. When we fear an unfair appraisal, it can distract us for weeks. When we are not accepted by our peers, we don't want to be around the team. When we feel taken advantage of, we can feel unappreciated and unmotivated. As Maslow eloquently put it, "Man doesn't live by bread alone, but when there is no bread, the need for bread can fully occupy your mind."

But once we have eaten the bread, once we are no longer dissatisfied with the lack of food or the poor appraisal process or the lack of upward mobility, these issues no longer have a dilatory effect on our performance. However, being "not dissatisfied" with the environment is not the same as being highly engaged with the challenges we face. Having a belly full of food doesn't make the job more interesting.

Limiting dissatisfaction is important but insufficient to facilitate engagement. Eliminating sources of dissatisfaction make it more likely that people will be willing and able to engage with opportunities that they deem worthy. Only after addressing basic need frustration in the environment, will most people be willing to learn, grow and take responsibility. We cannot expect the eliminating of frustrations, in and of themselves, to turn us on. Nor should we expect that people will learn and grow when their basic needs are frustrated. We need to work on both—in the right order.

When You Listen to the Stories People Tell, You'll Understand the Culture

People have an insatiable ability to complain about the environment, and we should be listening. It's important to understand that people tell stories (both true and untrue) because the stories are 1) important to them and 2) consistent with how they feel. Stories are the predominant way that an organization's culture is passed down generationally and the way that shared attitudes, beliefs, and behaviors are perpetuated, like a doctor using a stethoscope, listening to grumbles and metagrumbles will begin to tell you how people in your organization feel.

It would be short-sighted to react to everything we hear. However, the types of stories that people are telling can help clarify how the team feels about the present culture. If they are complaining that they don't have the ability to make simple decisions, you learn one thing. If they are talking about abusive, uncivil treatment, obviously, you have different issues. It is easy to want to avoid bitch sessions. No one wants to unnecessarily have negativity define our conversations. But once we realize that a certain amount of griping is unavoidable, then paying close attention to these grumbles can help us understand WHY people feel as they do so that we can better address cultural issues as we navigate our way into the future.

Avoid Becoming Competitively Disadvantaged

The jury is in. In the case of cooperation vs. competition, cooperation beats competition nearly every time except in the simplest, most mundane of activities. The research supporting more cooperative practices is overwhelming. Unfortunately, most organizations are not prepared to choose collaboration over internal competition.

Our belief in the positive effects of competition would be hard to overestimate. Make students compete to get an A. Who is the fastest person on the team? Top salesperson? High scorer? We like to talk about collaboration and teamwork, but often teamwork takes a back seat to our competitive instincts. Structurally, culturally, and philosophically, we are less prepared to collaborate than we might think. We are, after all, a nation that reveres all-stars.

We make rock stars out of individuals who 'win.' It doesn't matter if they are corporate raiders, actors, college athletes, or employees of the month. For most of our lives, we have been taught to compete, to stand out, to get the highest performance review, and to outperform our classmates. We have felt the thrill of victory and the agony of defeat in nearly every endeavor in which we have played a role.

Of course, we *say* we want teamwork. Most of us have been part of team-building exercises. We go away for weekends, we build little houses, we challenge our ability to trust as we fall out of trees, and even do improv in the hope that some of these collaborative skills will somehow find their way into team competencies when we return to the real world. We are not saying that this approach never works. However, in our experience, the transfer from the experiential training activity to life is rarer than we might like to think.

"Wait, don't people want to be more competitive? Aren't more competitive employees more effective employees?" Yes and no. Yes, some people like to be competitive, but recent research pegs that number at about a third of the people in most organizations. What this research also shows is that half of all employees prefer to collaborate if given a choice and that they are frustrated by processes that force people to compete with others on the team for a bonus, or a performance rating, or a promotion.

We need to learn to build more collaborative, cooperative structures. As we rely more heavily on teams, we will have to overcome our addiction to all-star cultures that unnecessarily limit the number of people who can win. It is probably true that the refinery manager in Elliot Carlyle's 1976 Harvard Business Review article, MacGregor, had a better idea. The next person promoted should not always be the all-star performer. It should be the person best able to lead and most helpful to other members of the team. After all, that will be his or her job as a leader at the next level. The best leaders are the people who make the rest of the team better.[7]

Don't Do for Others What they Can Do for Themselves

Recently, we had to wait 10 minutes to get a supervisor to approve a 10 percent military discount on a 25-dollar purchase. No exaggeration, a full 10 minutes. When he finally arrived at the register, the supervisor neither looked at the product nor checked our ID. He barely looked at the paper that he was signing. He just approved the transaction mindlessly. In what world does it make sense to trust the associate at the register with being the last contact in the customer experience, but not trust them to check the date on an ID card? Incidentally, the total discount was $2.50. What message are we communicating to people when we insist on employing a process that unequivocally implies that we don't trust them with a $2.50 decision?

We must stop doing for others what they can do for themselves. We need to trust more if we expect to be trusted in return. As leaders, we need to involve people in the planning and execution of the processes in which they work. People are more committed to and engaged in plans that they help create, but only if they are meaningfully involved. Involvement doesn't work if it is mere window dressing. Involvement begets higher levels of engagement when people have significant influence in the way work gets done without the interference of stupid rules that require them to seek permission to use common sense.

We are not arguing that we should not have controls. That would be absurd. However, if we are willing to risk our lives most days by traveling down the highway trusting that other cars will stay in their lane, then we should certainly be able to trust the people we hired to make decisions provided they have the pertinent information. To do otherwise is disrespectful and disengaging.

Do We Believe in the Potential of People (Redux)?

In nearly every case, the first step in creating an environment that supports engagement and commitment begins in the heart of the leader. Change requires leaders to take the first step before expecting others to follow. It requires that leaders believe that the motivation to learn and grow and contribute is natural, innate. It is easy to say, "I believe that ordinary people can produce great results." It is far more difficult to bet your career on the idea that you can create an environment where people will fully commit to the cause. We need to become more mindful of our beliefs, even those that we have not articulated, guide how we think about people, how we treat them and the practices we perpetuate in the process of trying to lead them.

Leadership on autopilot is not a good choice for most. Too many of our past practices have been designed based on a set of assumptions that are inconsistent with gaining people's trust and commitment. We might start by assessing our answers to the following questions and then doing an audit of our team's present practices.

- Are our choices and our practices consistent with our espoused values?
- Do we believe that it is important for people to feel safe and free of unnecessary fear? Or, do we believe that the fear that comes with most management practices is natural and actually works to motivate better performance?
- Do we believe that people have a strong need to connect, to belong, and to have trusting relationships on the team? Or, do we believe that these relationships are unnecessary and that performance is what matters?
- Do we believe that people need to feel appreciated? Or, do we feel that the paycheck is why people come

to work and how we express our appreciation for their efforts?

- Do we believe that people have an innate need to learn and grow and reach their potential? Or do we believe that people need to have an incentive to learn and that they will usually take the path of least resistance?
- Do we believe that people will sacrifice their personal needs to be part of a team engaged in a worthy cause? Or do we feel that people's behavior is primarily based on what they will personally gain by participating?

Leaders who lack confidence or who believe that people are like stationary objects that must be jump-started into action have very little chance of creating cultures that support people's need to grow. The only leaders who have a chance to build environments that gain commitment and support passionate involvement, are those who authentically believe that ordinary people are capable of making extraordinary, creative contributions.

One More Note about Pay

Our experience is consistent with most of the research about compensation. The best pay systems are fair and result in people thinking less about pay and more about what they hope to accomplish. We are not arguing that pay isn't important. It is important. If there is an incentive with enough pay at stake, it will motivate us to do what is necessary to get the money. But, as with most extrinsic manipulations described above, pay can turn out to be a costly distraction when individuals start to think about their paychecks instead of their contributions.

If we feel that we can't go without an incentive, we suggest that we focus on group awards. The larger the group, the better. Most metrics that attempt to evaluate the performance of the larger group tend to be fairer and more consistent with larger organizational goals. In some circumstances, the sharing of rewards or profits can even result in greater teamwork as people work toward the organization's success. (Think of stock options or profit/gain sharing.) If we need more collaboration, then it really doesn't make much sense for one group to win in the incentive pay lottery while the organization as a whole loses. Why can't we all win and lose—as a team? After all, in today's networked, democratized world, little gets accomplished by individuals without the help of others. *In the best pay practices, everyone gets an opportunity to win and one person's success should not necessitate another's failure.*

Chapter 7 | Summary

10 Rules for Creating an Environment that Supports Engagement

1. Stop the motivational insanity. Lessen your reliance on "if you do this, you will get that" incentives. They destroy interest, undermine learning and creativity, and create fear.
2. Stop trying to motivate people. You can't motivate them. People are born motivated. Motivation is a choice. Leaders only create compelling opportunities in which the best people are more likely to choose to fully engage in the process. Leaders are in the invitation and opportunity business. The motivation of others is not their responsibility.
3. Create an environment that helps to satisfy people's needs for security, fairness, connection, and appreciation. Until people's basic needs are largely satisfied, learning and growth are unlikely. Eliminating the causes of basic need dissatisfaction is a continual process that requires that we continue to monitor how people feel and the stories they tell.
4. Ensure that every person has a compelling opportunity to learn, grow, and reach his or her potential. Review the design of jobs as well as job performance. Ensure that learning is part of every job. We have never seen a person who is actively learning and turned off. We have seen many bright and talented people become bored and create problems.
5. Recruit people who share your passion and your values. One of the most underappreciated secrets to

great leadership is the ability to ensure that only those people who share the team's values are allowed on the team. A large number of the motivation problems that leaders face are created because the wrong people are on the team and they have no interest in what the team is trying to accomplish.

6. Get rid of leaders who don't believe it is possible to create high engagement cultures. They tend to resist leadership innovation and advocate practices that give managers more control. These leaders tend to undermine engagement efforts. They make commitment less likely. They frustrate people's basic needs. They create unnecessary fear. People deserve better.
7. Don't do for others what they can do for themselves. High levels of engagement require less powerful leaders. We need to ensure that we don't communicate, even unintentionally, that people are not in control of the processes in which they work. People are simply more committed to what they help create. People must be involved in both the design, planning, and execution of the work.
8. Create a TO-STOP list. When it comes to motivation, more can be less. We need to get rid of any process or practice that gets in the way of the natural motivation of people. People want to make a difference. As we become more mindful of the unintended effects of the processes that we have inherited from the past, we will begin to see just how much of the fear and demotivation on many teams is a predictable consequence of management practices that were designed to ensure managerial control.

9. Change the stories people tell. The stories people tell may not always be accurate, but listening to them can be the best way to accurately assess how people feel and what's important to them. We will know that things are changing when people begin to tell different stories.
10. Involve everyone. Creating a better environment is everyone's responsibility. Leaders can't create the environment alone. The team must become mutually accountable for the creation of the culture. If culture is a reflection of a team's habits, then it will require the involvement of the entire team to change it.

Embrace Vulnerability

> *"Vulnerability is the birthplace of love, belonging, joy, courage, empathy, and creativity. It is the source of hope, empathy, accountability, and authenticity. If we want greater clarity in our purpose or deeper and more meaningful spiritual lives, vulnerability is the path."*
>
> *– Brené Brown*

Sh** happens, no matter how much we wish otherwise. Trying to control the uncontrollable is a fool's errand. It produces athletes who suffer performance anxiety and leaders who become our biggest nightmares. Over-control robs people of the joy inherent in creating something new. Trying to never make a mistake is a mistake. If you are not uncomfortable and making mistakes, chances are you are not doing anything very interesting. Chances are you are playing it so safe that innovation and learning are things you talk about but rarely experience. To build the kind of cultures advocated in this book, we must first learn to accept the fact that we don't have the answers. We must be willing to take unpopular stances even if we are standing alone. We will have to develop the courage to enter the fray without a defined roadmap and a fistful of answers.

Building cultures that fully engage people will require that we embrace our vulnerability. We will have to embrace a level of uncertainty, risk, and emotional exposure that is certain to make even the most confident among us uncomfortable. For, when we choose to admit that we need help, we make it far more likely that others will respond in kind.

The expression of vulnerability changes us. It changes how we think and the risks we are willing to take. When we choose a more vulnerable path, we communicate to others that they are trusted, and valued. It enhances our ability to connect, increases our sense of belonging, and makes it far more likely that people will take the risk to be more authentic. In our hearts we know that we cannot expect loyalty if we are not loyal. We cannot expect to be trusted if we are not trusting. Being the first to say "I love you" may be risky, but it does increase the likelihood that people will be more authentic in their responses. When we invest in relationships without knowing whether they will work out, we make it more likely that we will make an emotional connection. Furthermore, learning is accelerated when we understand that no one believes that they have "the answer." The expression of vulnerability is a visible manifestation of our belief that we may be imperfect but that we are deserving of trust and respect, that we can't succeed alone, and that it's not all about us.

To be real, vulnerability can be hazardous to your organizational health. It would be nice to say that being vulnerable, embracing uncertainty, and advocating change are devoid of serious risk, but that would be nonsense. Too many people are rewarded in organizations for having the answer—usually based on what has been successful in the past. Organizations often value the appearance of strength and confidence more than they do humility. First graders who appear attentive and raise their hands more frequently are treated as smarter students. Confident little league players make the all-star team. Honor students get special perks. Make a confident presentation in a meeting, and you might join the top salesperson on the promotion list. As your career progresses and you are identified as a "high performer," you might get access to special elevators, preferred parking spots, and maybe even an eating area where "less successful people" are not invited. The societal message is clear. We value all-stars. We especially value them if they are willing to conform to present cultural norms. Appearance matters. We don't appreciate leaders who appear weak, who lack charisma, or who are so different that they challenge our collective beliefs. No wonder most leaders are reluctant to appear understated or too different, or too vulnerable.

The good news, however, is that a time is quickly approaching when humility and vulnerability will be seen for what they are—prerequisites to building great teams. When that time comes, the illusion of certainty will be seen as life-threatening to the organization, and innovation and engagement will finally be recognized as the primary sources of competitive advantage. Love, higher expectations, and mutual accountability will become more the norm as we realize that cultures that reward bravado over humility, and certainty over vulnerability, are too costly to perpetuate.

It's not about Me

Every time we visit Give Kids the World and its CEO, Pam Landwirth, it is life-altering. The love, compassion, and laughter that resonate from the Village stand in stark contrast to the sadness that must accompany every guest whose terminally or critically ill child explores one of the most unique experiences on the planet. Although we had visited many times before, we were eager to see the innovations that had resulted in GKTW having been celebrated as the world's best-run charity several years running.

The "Kid's Village," as it's known, is a magical place, at least as magical as Disney's Magic Kingdom, located just a few miles down the road. The Kid's Village, founded by Auschwitz survivor and hotelier Henri Landwirth, was built to provide a cost-free, week-long experience for thousands of families each year, many of whom are braving the most trying time in their lives.

We were determined not to cry on this visit as we had in the past. It didn't work this time either. Each time we visit, our teary-eyed reactions are overshadowed by the joy radiating from the smiles of the children and their families. We are always amazed by the positive emotion that flows from guests and staff. The extraordinary challenges faced by these families seem somehow to take a back seat for a week. The optimism and enthusiasm of the GKTW team create an experience that you have to see to believe.

Staff members, including volunteers (more than 7,000 hours are contributed in a normal week), are so engaged, so committed, and so empathetic that it is contagious. You can't help but want to enlist. It is that special.

As we greeted Pam in her office at The Village, it became immediately apparent once again why there was a waiting list to volunteer. She wore her love for the children and her love for the GKTW team on her sleeve. She always does. (Yes, she too unabashedly uses the word love when she describes how the team feels about each other.)

Entering her office, we were struck by a sign that she had hung by the door. It said simply, "It's not about me." Pam told us that it was just a simple reminder that "as leaders, we need to remember that we are not the show. We serve the people who put on the show for our GUESTS. The Village is a special place because every member of our team treats every interaction with our guests as an opportunity to enrich their lives. It's about the families. It's about the team. It's not about me."

We have known Pam for decades. She could read in our eyes that we were about to ask a question, but before we could ask, she continued, "In our society, it's too easy for leaders who are experienced to begin to believe that they have the answers. We may have more experience. But it is important that we remember that we don't have all the answers."

She went on to remind us that most organizational cultures value leaders who appear strong and charismatic. These are all-star-driven cultures where visibly solving the problem, having the best idea, and giving the best speech are valued significantly more than humility, connection, and empathy. For her, the 'it's not about me' sign was just a reminder to take time to ensure that she remained grounded, mindful of her mission, mindful of her responsibility to enable others, and mindful of how "lucky she is to have the opportunity to serve."

We were taken aback, not so much by the sign or Pam's reasoning but by the fact that the most humble leader we knew felt that she needed a reminder to be humble. Then again, maybe the sign was just evidence that genuinely humble leaders work hard to ensure that they remain humble and not distracted by their successes.

Pam's example stands as a reminder to all that humility and vulnerability are not signs of weakness. They are signs of confidence, strength, and courage. As with all acts of courage, they evolve from an awareness of what it means to lead. Humility, open-mindedness, and vulnerability are not leadership tactics to Pam. They are an expression of who she is and what she stands for. Pam's actions clearly communicate that she believes that the team's ability is enhanced when all members of the group, not just its leader, have the power to influence the future.

Perhaps, we should all have a sign in our lives that reminds us that it is not all about us. Based on Pam's simple sign and her passionate beliefs, we piggy-backed on her example to create our own reminder:

It's not about me. Leadership is being in service to others.

It's not about me. Leadership is about loving others.

It's not about me. It's about the CAUSE that binds us together.

It's not about me. It's about doing something remarkable together that we could never do alone.

It's not about me. It's about the promises that we make to each other.

It's not about me. It's about our team.

Thank you, Pam.

When Words are a Window to Our Souls

Be more vulnerable. Be honest. Don't let your past dictate your future. Become more self-aware. At their core, these are simple suggestions to understand. However, building cultures that support people's willingness to actualize these traits will require a significant change for most. There isn't a good road map showing how to change hundreds of years of tradition in order to embrace the kind of people-centric cultures that we have talked about for the better part of the last century. Embracing our vulnerability is a good place to start, however. Wouldn't we all be better off if, a little more often, we learned to authentically say:

- I don't have the answer,
- I have changed my mind,
- I am sorry,
- Thank you for your help and support?

These simple statements communicate that we are vulnerable, that we don't have the answer. At the same time, they exude a passion for our cause and our love for people, likely freeing others to do the same. Our expression of vulnerability is likely to be contagious. As every member of the team embraces the idea that no one has the answer and that we are stronger when we act together, only then are we likely to become a team. Only then will our collective abilities far exceed what we could have accomplished individually. Our collective, humble recognition of our limitations frees us to accomplish things that might have seemed impossible when our journey began. Certainly, Orlando hotelier Henri Landwirth had no idea when he envisioned helping sick children that he would build a Kid's Village and bring joy to more than 5,000 families a year. He could not have known that he would meet and marry a humble, remarkable leader capable of changing the world with her passion.

Vulnerability is a strength. It is a prerequisite to engagement. It tells everyone that we are part of the team, not apart from it. It invites ideas and challenges. It says that we embrace our humanness. It tells the world that it is "not all about us." It is a prerequisite to loving others.

It's Time to Choose

Say out loud, "I want to be more vulnerable and connected." Can you feel it?

Now, say out loud, "I choose to be vulnerable and connected."

The two statements are fundamentally different. "I want" is a passive statement of intention. Choosing, on the other hand, is active. It signals that the decision has been made, that we have chosen to take a different path. Choosing communicates an entirely different level of commitment. If we are to be successful, simply wanting to be different will not be sufficient.

People need their leaders to choose, to be ALL IN. They want to know that we will have their backs and that we are not going to fold at the first sign of resistance.

In this book, we have advocated that leaders consider a number of choices that we believe are necessary to build cultures in which people are willing to engage and act creatively. We hope that a few of these ideas will help you create dialogues that accelerate the changes that you hope to facilitate. We believe strongly that, as leaders in organizations, we have a responsibility to do more than just create teams that consistently win. We believe that we have a responsibility to create cultures where work is not a four letter word, where education really does facilitate learning, and where athletics are a means to teach life lessons.

We strongly believe that cultures that support engagement and creativity are fostered when we:

- Choose to lead from LOVE and not FEAR,
- Choose to create a SHARED CAUSE worthy of commitment,
- Choose to EXPECT REMARKABLE from every person regardless of position,
- Choose to be MUTUALLY ACCOUNTABLE for our performance,
- Choose to LEARN TO LOVE DIFFERENT, especially things that make us uncomfortable,

- Choose to seek COMMITMENT, NOT COMPLIANCE, because there is no such thing as passionate obedience; and
- Choose to embrace our VULNERABILITY, because nobody wants to engage when the leader of the group appears to have all the answers.

We don't believe that making these choices will make a leader successful. Nor do we think that this is a complete list of the choices that distinguish great leaders from the rest. We do believe, however, that making more of these choices will have a positive impact on how people react to our influence. We have a responsibility to create more exemplars, more people willing to take responsibility for doing the right thing even when the expedient thing is easier. God knows, we need more exemplars in a world where more and more people seem to worship at the altar of 'win at all costs' and 'the end justifies the means.' We have the ability and the means to create cultures in which people can not only 'win more games' but can feel better about winning those games because, in the process of winning, they will have learned and grown and reached closer to their potentials. When we are better leaders, we impact our communities in ways that we often don't realize. When people feel like they are learning and growing, they are not only better team players, but inevitably, they become better fathers, mothers, brothers, sisters, neighbors, and citizens.

Leadership is a responsibility. It begins with a choice to do something meaningful and to engage others in the process. It is less a matter of style and more a matter of the heart. It is a responsibility to serve others by creating a culture in which people can choose to do the remarkable and serve others in the process. For those of us who believe that this is a worthy calling, our time has come.

What does love have to do with it? Just about everything.

Endnotes

Introduction: What Does Love Have to Do with It?

[1] Mann, A., & Harter, J. (2016). *The worldwide employee engagement crisis.* Gallup Business Journal, 7.

[2] McKinsey & Company. (2016). *Digital strategy: the economics of disruption.* McKinsey Quarterly, 2.

[3] Kellerman, B. (2012). *The end of leadership.* HarperBusiness.

1. Choose Love, Not Fear

[1] Kirshner, A. (2017, January 10). *Watch Dabo Swinney's emotional interview after Clemson beat Alabama.* Retrieved from https://www.sbnation.com/college-football/2017/1/10/14221956/dabo-swinney-interview-postgame-national-championship-clemson-alabama.

[2] Jones, T. (2019, August 28). *Tom Jones: welcome, Dabo; now cool it a little.* Retrieved from https://www.tampabay.com/sports/college/jones-hey-dabo-tone-down-that-greatest-love-of-all-shtick/2309225.

[3] Wilson, G. & Robinson, M. (2006–2007). *Love and fear, entelechy, fall /winter, no.8.*

[4] Mann, A., & Harter, J. (2016). *The worldwide employee engagement crisis.* Gallup Business Journal, 7.

[5] Gallup. (2016). *How millennials want to work and live: the six big changes leaders have to make.* Retrieved from https://www.gallup.com/workplace/238073/millennials-work-live.aspx.

[6] Councils, G. A. (2015). *Outlook on the Global Agenda 2015.* In World Economic Forum.

[7] (2015, April 17). *Leadership across cultures.* Retrieved from https://hbr.org/2015/05/leadership-across-cultures.

[8] (2018). *2018 Edelman trust barometer.* Edelman. Annual Global Study, 2018. Retrieved from https://www.edelman.com/sitcs/g/files/aatuss191/files/2018-10/2018_Edelman_Trust_Barometer_Global_Report_FEB.pdf.

[9] Cuddy, A. J., Fiske, S. T., & Glick, P. (2008). *Warmth and competence as universal dimensions of social perception: the stereotype content model and the BIAS map.* Advances in experimental social psychology, 40, 61–149.

[10] Zenger, J., & Folkman, J. (2014, August 7). *I'm the boss! Why should I care if you like me?* Retrieved from https://hbr.org/2013/05/im-the-boss-why-should-i-care.

2. Create a Cause Worthy of Commitment

[1] Frankl, V. E. (1984). *Man's search for meaning: an introduction to logotherapy.* New York: Simon & Schuster.

[2] Maslow, A. H. (1965). *Eupsychian management: a journal.* Homewood, Ill: R.D. Irwin.

[3] Frost, C. F. (1996). *Changing forever: the well-kept secret of America's leading companies.* East Lansing, MI: Michigan State University Press.

Frost, C. F., Wakeley, J. H., & Ruh, R. A. (1974). *The Scanlon Plan for organization development: identity, participation, and equity.* Michigan State University Press.

[4] DePree, M. (2011). *Leadership is an art.* Currency.

De Pree, M. (2008). *Leadership jazz: the essential elements of a great leader.* Crown Business.

3. Get the Right People On the Team and the Wrong People Off

[1] Collins, J. C. (2001). *Good to great: why some companies make the leap... and others don't.* New York, NY: Harper Business.

[2] Sutton, R. I. (2007). *The no asshole rule: building a civilized workplace and surviving one that isn't.* New York: Warner Business Books.

[3] Porath, C., & Pearson, C. (2013). *The price of incivility.* Harvard business review, 91(1–2), 115–121.

4. Dare to Expect Remarkable

[1] Oberlander, A. A. (1963). *The collective conscience in recruiting.* In address to Life Insurance Agency Management Association annual meeting, Chicago, Illinois (p. 5).

[2] Livingston, J. S. (2016, November 15). *Pygmalion in management.* Retrieved from https://hbr.org/2003/01/pygmalion-in-management.

[3] Rosenthal, R., & Jacobson, L. (1968). *Pygmalion in the classroom.* The urban review, 3(1), 16–20.

[4] Mehrabian, A., & Weiner, M. (1967). *Decoding of inconsistent communications.* Journal of Personality and Social Psychology, 6, 109–114.

Mehrabian, A., & Ferris, S. (1967). *Inference of attitudes from nonverbal communication in two channels.* Journal of Consulting Psychology, 31, 248–252.

[5] Argyle, M. (1972). *Non-verbal communication in human social interaction.* In R. A. Hinde, Non-verbal communication. Oxford, England: Cambridge U. Press.

[6] Livingston, J. S. (2016, November 15). *Pygmalion in management.* Retrieved from https://hbr.org/2003/01/pygmalion-in-management.

[7] Rosenthal, R., & Fode, K. L. (1963). *The effect of experimenter bias on the performance of the albino rat.* Behavioral Science, 8(3), 183–189.

[8] Atkinson, J. W. (1957). *Motivational determinants of risk-taking behavior.* Psychological review, 64(6p1), 359.

McClelland, D. C., Atkinson, J. W., Clark, R. A., & Lowell, E. L. (1976). *The achievement motive.*

[9] Schein, E. H. (2010). Organizational culture and leadership (Vol. 2). John Wiley & Sons.

[10] Barham, J. A., & Thomas, A. (2018, September 18). *Jaime Escalante in the 21st century: still standing and delivering.* Retrieved from https://thebestschools.org/magazine/jaime-escalante-21st-century-still-standing-delivering/.

5. Make Accountability Mutual

[1] DePree, M. (2011). *Leadership is an art.* Currency.

[2] (2016). *UNC women's soccer coach Anson Dorrance covets culture over championships.* The Daily Tarheel. Retrieved from https://www.dailytarheel.com/article/2016/11/unc-womens-soccer-coach-anson-dorrance-covets-culture-over-championships.

[3] Kanter, R. M. (2006). *Confidence: how winning streaks and losing streaks begin and end.* Crown Business.

[4] (n.d.). *Interview with Ambassador Winston Lord.* Retrieved from https://nsarchive2.gwu.edu//coldwar/interviews/episode-15/lord1.html.

[5] Shahid, S. (2015). *Lack of leadership. Outlook on the global agenda.* Retrieved from http://reports.weforum.org/outlook-global-agenda-2015/top-10-trends-of-2015/3-lack-of-leadership/.

[6] McGregor, D. (1957). *An uneasy look at performance appraisals.* Harvard Business Review, Vol. 35 No. 3, pp. 89–95.

[7] Maslow, A. H., Frager, R., Fadiman, J., McReynolds, C., & Cox, R. (1970). *Motivation and personality.* Harper & Row New York. McClelland, DC, & Burnham, DH (1976). Power is the great motivator. Harvard Business Review, 25, 159–166.

6. Learn to Love Different

[1] Contributor: On Marketing. (2012, August 8). *The real story behind Apple's 'think different' campaign.* Retrieved from https://www.forbes.com/sites/onmarketing/2011/12/14/the-real-story-behind-apples-think-different-campaign/#3ae94d3e62ab.

[2] Mayer, R. C., Warr, R. S., & Zhao, J. (2018). *Do pro-diversity policies improve corporate innovation?* Financial Management, 47(3), 617–650.

[3] Lorenzo, R., Voigt, N., Schetelig, K., Zawadzki, A., Welpe, I., & Brosi, P. (2017). *The mix that matters, innovation through diversity.* The Boston Consulting Group.

[4] Hunt, V., Prince, S., Dixon-Fyle, S., & Yee, L. (2018). *Delivering through diversity.* Mckinsey & Company. Retrieved July 26, 2018.

[5] Frauenheim, E., & Lewis-Kulin, S. (2016). *Pursuing the potential of all employees.* Great Place to Work.

[6] Gompers, P., and Kovvali, S. *The other diversity dividend.* Harvard Business Review 96, no. 4 (July–August 2018): 72–77.

[7] Dweck, C. S. (2008). *Mindset: the new psychology of success.* Random House Digital, Inc.

[8] Stack, J., & Burlingham, B. (2003). *A stake in the outcome: building a culture of ownership for the long-term success of your business.* Broadway Business.

[9] Case, J. (1997). *Opening the books.* Harvard Business Review, 75(2), 118–128.

[10] Carlzon, J., & Peters, T. (1987). *Moments of truth.* Cambridge, MA: Ballinger.

[11] Nededog, J. (2016, June 30). *'Full Frontal' producer talks the hiring process for one of TV's most diverse writing staffs.* Retrieved from https://www.businessinsider.com/how-samantha-bee-found-her-diverse-writing-team-2016-6.

7. Seek Commitment, Not Compliance

[1] Kohn, A. (1999). *Punished by rewards: the trouble with gold Stars, incentive plans, A's, praise, and other bribes.* Houghton Mifflin Harcourt.

[2] Deci, E. L., Koestner, R., & Ryan, R. M. (1999). *A meta-analytic review of experiments examining the effects of extrinsic rewards on intrinsic motivation.* Psychological bulletin, 125(6), 627.

[3] Kohn, A. (1999). *Punished by rewards: the trouble with gold stars, incentive plans, A's, praise, and other bribes.* Houghton Mifflin Harcourt.

[4] McGregor, D. (1966). *The human side of enterprise.*

[5] Fowler, G. A. (2011, September 8). *For 40 Years, an advocate for the underclass.* Retrieved from https://www.wsj.com/articles/SB10001424053111904537404576554790064918716.

[6] Frankl, V. E. (1985). *Man's search for meaning.* Simon and Schuster.

[7] Carlisle, A. E. (1976). *MacGregor.* Organizational Dynamics, 5(1), 50–62.

About the Authors

Gary Heil

Gary Heil is an author, educator, lawyer, consultant, and coach. For the last four decades, he has been an ardent student of the human side of organizations. He was a pioneer in the study of employee engagement and loyal customer relationships, and he remains a vocal and passionate advocate for finding more effective ways to lead inspired teams.

Gary is the co-founder of the Center for Innovative Leadership, where he continues to advise leaders in a wide range of industries on cultural issues. He has served on a number of public and private Boards including Gymboree, Red Envelope and Front Range Solutions and presently serves as the Chairman of the Board of CellTech Metals.

Gary has spent the last decade engaged in a study of more than 700 leaders trying to better ascertain why many leaders have difficulty making the rhetoric of better leadership a reality and what separates exemplary leaders and inspired teams from the merely good ones. The results of this study are the basis for the book *Choose Love, Not Fear.*

He is the co-author of a number of best-selling books including *Leadership and the Customer Revolution*, *One Size Fits One*, *Maslow on Management*, *The Leader's New Clothes*, and *Revisiting the Human Side of Enterprise.*

Gary's journey has been a diverse one. In addition to his consulting and coaching roles, he was the co-founder and CEO of the National Pitching Association where he teamed up with a number of Hall of Fame players and coaches to help young athletes play more effectively without injury. He has served as an Examiner for the Malcolm Baldrige National Quality Award and as SafeLife's Chief Marketing and Strategy Officer. He co-founded the webcast Leadership Lessons from the Fast Lane and early in his career, he navigated a Polar icebreaker from pole to pole.

He is a graduate of the United States Coast Guard Academy. He received a Masters degree in Organizational Behavior and a Juris Doctor degree from The University of California, Hastings College of Law.

Ryan Heil, PhD

Dr. Ryan Heil, the Chief People & Culture Officer for the Washington Speakers Bureau, specializes in assessing and developing organizational cultures that help make workplaces more collaborative, creative, and productive. Through his experiences and research in both college athletics and the private sector, he developed a new, more accurate, and more expeditious method to assess an organization or team's culture.

As a player, coach, administrator, and researcher, Dr. Heil has spent more than 15 years working in and researching college athletics and has a unique understanding of the changing landscape of the Division I level. Moreover, when combined with his experience as the Chief of Staff for the VP of Student Affairs at Clemson University, he has an intimate understanding of the role athletics plays in the higher education community.

Dr. Heil has also served as the Chief Marketing Officer of Zipbuds Inc. where he led a company-wide transformation overhauling communication and sales strategies and helping the development team to design, develop, fund and source new products.

Ryan received his Ph.D. in Educational Leadership and his master's degree in Clinical Mental Health Counseling from Clemson University. He was awarded his B.S. from Lewis-Clark State College. A former D1 baseball player and college baseball coach, Ryan also played professional baseball in the New York Mets organization.

Acknowledgments

Many people helped us write this book—not all knowingly. We owe much to those that came before us and to the many exemplary leaders who demonstrate that choosing to lead with positive emotion is not only more effective, but also highly rewarding. Some of these leaders are highlighted in this book. Many are not. We thank all of you for challenging us and for showing us that there is a better, more human way to lead. We are in your debt.

In every journey, there are a few people whose influence shapes our beliefs. In many cases, these 'leaders' are probably unaware of their effect on us. Dabo Swinney, Clemson's Football Coach, is a force. His positivity and love for people led us to view our experiences differently. Through the force of his example, we began to more fully understand the advice given to us decades earlier by president and CEO of SAS Jan Carlzon. Love or Fear? It is the first choice a leader must knowingly or unknowingly make.

This book began nearly a decade ago when our colleague David Kyle worked with us to begin interviewing leaders. David helped us gain perspective and challenged us to see the world differently. He did for us what he had done for the leaders that he has coached in Silicon Valley for decades: he made us better.

Deborah Stephens urged Gary to write his first book nearly thirty years ago and her fingerprints are all over this one. She worked with us as we refined our learnings and our message. She encouraged us and told us when she saw us missing the mark. We want to thank her, not only for her contributions to this tome, but for a career full of support and guidance.

Laura Pyne, our editor, friend, and at times, team leader is simply a force of nature. Her energy and enthusiasm is contagious. Her constructive feedback, invaluable. Laura has much to say about these issues in her own right. We only hope we can support her as she has supported us.

Harry Rhoads, Founder of WSB, has been our advisor and friend forever. His mark on this book may not be visible to the reader but his wisdom continues to inform our thinking and his example demonstrates what is possible when love wins out over fear.

We would also like to thank Michaela Heil for reading draft after draft without complaint and for her lawyer-like (literally) analysis of our logic.

And a special thank you to our leader, Carol Heil. Her love and support kept this book on track. Her wisdom made it more understandable and relatable. Her patience with the two of us uncommon. Her contributions gave this project meaning.